D0117212

God Knows You're Grieving

God Knows You're Stressed:
Simple Ways to Restore Your Balance

God Knows You'd Like a New Body:
12 Ways to Befriend the One You've Got

God Knows You're Grieving

Things to do to help you through

Joan Guntzelman

SORIN BOOKS   Notre Dame, IN

For his challenging and provocative mind,

for his long-time help and support,

and mostly for his good and loving heart,

this book is dedicated in gratitiude to

Denis Hines.

As publisher of the *GOD KNOWS* series, SORIN BOOKS is dedicated to providing resources to assist readers to enhance their quality of life. We welcome your comments and suggestions, which may be conveyed to:

SORIN BOOKS
P.O. Box 1006
Notre Dame, IN 46556-1006
Fax: 1-800-282-5681
e-mail: sorinbk@nd.edu

BV
4905.2
.G86
2001

© 2001 by Joan Guntzelman

www.sorinbooks.com

International Standard Book Number: 1-893732-39-8

Cover and text design by Katherine Robinson Coleman

Printed and bound in the United States of America

Library of Congress Cataloging-in-Publication Data
Guntzelman, Joan, 1937-
God knows you're grieving : things to do to help you through /
Joan Guntzelman.
     p. cm.
     ISBN 1-893732-39-8 (pbk.)
     1. Grief--Religious aspects--Christianity. I. Title.
BV4905.2 .G86 2001
248.8'66--dc21
                              2001002437
                                 CIP

CONTENTS

Introduction

"There is nothing permanent in life except change."

What the Greek philosopher Heraclitus meant when he spoke these words over 2,500 years ago was that nothing remains the same. In our minds this is something we know well. Yet, despite every person's experience, we hold tight to the notion that we should be able to make it through life without having to lose anything or anyone. Then, when a significant loss does come to us, we are devastated.

Such loss plunges us into rough and unknown waters that crash about and within us, tossing us like driftwood. The upheaval and movement feel uncontrollable. Waves of anxiety wash over us with unimaginable force until we feel there is no way out. We feel like we're drowning. Sometimes we would rather give ourselves up and sink into the pain. We'd prefer to die. Nothing seems to have such power with us as experiences like these of loss and death. We feel like life is over, like we're dying ourselves, like we'll never be whole again.

Grieving is the natural way we go about adjusting to loss. It's the way we gradually come to know deep within ourselves—whether we like it or not—that the loss is real. Being cast about on the waves of grief begins to serve its purpose. Despite all the distress, painful emotion, and change, despite the ache in our hearts and often even in our bodies, we gradually come to pull our lives back together again. Though the loss may never be what we would choose, we begin to find that we can make it, we can go on with our lives. Through all the pain healing is possible.

Twelve Ways of Grieving

*G*od Knows You're Grieving is intended as a source of support—when loss and grief enter your life and threaten to overwhelm you. While nothing—including this book—can remove the pain of the experience, help is always available. Sometimes help comes when we find a better way to understand what we're feeling. A prayer, sacred writings, some words of wisdom, or a story from someone who's been there can touch our hearts. Sometimes we find direction from another person that offers a perspective or approach that we've never even considered.

The twelve ways of grieving described in this book are meant to offer suggestions and support as we travel our own journeys through grief and loss. They may be helpful in sequence, or you may find a particular way that speaks to your situation at a given moment. Each way addresses some aspect of the grieving experience and offers suggestions that others have found helpful in their own grieving. You may find yourself moving around through the ways in no particular order, using whatever speaks to you at any moment.

No two experiences of loss are the same, nor are two experiences of grieving. Just as each relationship is unique, so is the grieving that follows its loss. So while many people may have similar experiences, don't expect to follow another's experience exactly. Allow room for your own journey.

When you find a quote or a story that resonates with your experience, stay with it for a while. Sit with it and savor it. Let it rumble around in your mind. Find the part in it that seems just right for you and think about it in relation to your own loss. Let your emotions flow. Write in your journal about your experience. Keep this writing for yourself. Write a letter to the dear one you lost. Let the experience be part of your prayer.

Except for the long stories for which the author is noted, I have changed the names of the storytellers that are quoted in the book. Each storyteller offers rich wisdom. They have been caught up in the journey through grief. Perhaps one of the stories in the book will provoke you to write a story of your own. There are no simple directions or right ways to grieve. What works is what helps you move towards health and wholeness.

Remember, the grieving process is not prone to quick fixes. When we grieve, we are involved completely in the process. Who or what we lost, what else is going on in our lives at the time, our own patterns and past experiences of loss, and many other factors will play roles in this particular time. We do have choices. Each experience of loss can lead to new life and growth—even through all its pain and sorrow—or can bring us down. The choice is ours. In the book of Deuteronomy in the Hebrew scriptures, Moses challenged the people of that day. In a similar way, we are challenged when we face loss. Moses said, "I set before you today life and death. Choose life." The choice for us is the same.

1

Realize That You Are Under Assault and Healing Takes Time

TO EXPERIENCE SOME HEALING
WITHIN OURSELVES, AND TO CON-
TRIBUTE HEALING TO THE WORLD,
WE ARE SUMMONED TO WADE
THROUGH THE MUCK FROM TIME
TO TIME. WHERE WE DO NOT GO
WILLINGLY, SOONER OR LATER WE
WILL BE DRAGGED.

James Hollis

When a loss of some magnitude comes into our lives, the accompanying grief threatens to swallow us up no matter what we do to avoid it. Early in our loss, we try to block out the grief and pretend it is not so. Months after the sudden death of her husband in an accident at work, Carolyn asked one day, "Do you think there could have been a mistake, and maybe the man who died wasn't my husband? Maybe he just was dazed from the accident and is out wandering around and can't find his way home."

Grief is a time of being undone. We feel our whole world fall apart. We feel out of control. Physically we may be exhausted, sigh a lot, want to sleep all the time (or be unable to sleep), and feel like we have a constant lump in our throat or hole in our stomach. We either eat too much or not at all. We may even be physically sick. Our emotions come and go as numbness takes over, and we walk around in a daze. Then the sadness wells up, and we dissolve again. We keep ourselves so busy that we don't have time to think about our problem. When we do, we may feel like we want to die.

We resist what's happening. We fight it, can't believe it, look for someone to rescue us, look for a magic cure, and do anything but accept it. We're just built that way. In some situations—for example, when we are sick or when we lost a job—our fighting the loss may help. It may give us the strength to find a solution to the problem. All the resistance in the world is natural for us when our lives feel like they are falling apart.

However, when our loss is the death or impending death of someone dear or the breakup of a relationship, our resistance and fight cannot change what is. Resistance may help us for a little while and may even be our first step in coming to grips with the reality. But, to keep fighting after we've reached a certain point can be fruitless and begin to work against us.

Often the best we can do when we come to this point is to let it be. We *are* under assault. And, this is an assault that we can't "fix." Most of us have become adept at finding quick solutions to problems and thinking that we can manage most of what comes our way. We might even think something is wrong with us if we can't fix our grief quickly. We've come to expect that we can control just about everything.

Grief and loss are experiences that can't be solved. When loss comes into our lives, it's time to open ourselves to the experience of our own helplessness. We can control many things in life, but not this one. Grief simply is the way we humans are affected by loss. We must learn to allow the experience.

We need to know that we won't be feeling like this forever, even though we are incapable of comprehending this truth emotionally. Big changes and adjustments are going on within us.

If we give ourselves to grieving, we will gradually make our way. The key here is to *give* ourselves to it. In fact, healing comes by journeying right through the pain of loss, not by trying to sidestep it. Healing won't happen quickly. The time of healing tends to be in proportion to the significance of who or what we lost. As a result, only small losses are grieved and healed quickly.

Above all, as we grieve, we must be gentle and loving with ourselves. Nothing is accomplished by harshness. We may feel thoroughly alone, abandoned by everyone, including God. Yet, whether we know it or not, believe it or not, feel it or not, God—by definition, all-present—is as close as our breath and wraps us in love.

DO NOT BE AFRAID, FOR I HAVE REDEEMED YOU; I HAVE CALLED YOU BY YOUR NAME, YOU ARE MINE. SHOULD YOU PASS THROUGH THE WATERS, I SHALL BE WITH YOU; OR THROUGH RIVERS, THEY WILL NOT SWALLOW YOU UP. SHOULD YOU WALK THROUGH FIRE, YOU WILL NOT SUFFER, AND THE FLAME WILL NOT BURN YOU. FOR I AM YAHWEH, YOUR GOD, THE HOLY ONE OF ISRAEL, YOUR SAVIOR.

The Prophet Isaiah

Realize That You Are Under Assault and Healing Takes Time

- Remember this affirmation and speak it to yourself several times each day: "My grief is part of my loss. I can stay with my grief and allow myself to feel it."

- Allow your feelings to come to the surface without fighting them. You might talk with your feelings, welcome them, and ask for their wisdom. You might also talk honestly about your experience and about what you are feeling with someone who is a good listener, a person who won't tell you what you should or shouldn't feel.

- When your experience feels overwhelming, simply be with it, knowing that it won't last forever. Sometimes we just need to let it be.

- A paraphrase of an old prayer says, "God, help me to fight when I need to fight and accept when I need to accept, and the wisdom to know the difference." Ask for that wisdom. Ask for the strength to do both those things well. Learn to trust the life process and know the times when we should submit to it.

I LEARNED GRADUALLY THAT THE DEEPER WE PLUNGE INTO SUFFERING, THE DEEPER WE CAN ENTER INTO A NEW, AND DIFFERENT, LIFE——A LIFE NO WORSE THAN BEFORE AND SOMETIMES BETTER. A WILLINGNESS TO FACE THE LOSS AND TO ENTER INTO THE DARKNESS IS THE FIRST STEP WE MUST TAKE. LIKE

ALL FIRST STEPS, IT IS PROBABLY THE
MOST DIFFICULT AND TAKES THE
MOST TIME.

Gerald L. Sittser

Marathon

Jim was slouched down in the embrace of a deeply cushioned chair, his long legs stretched out before him. His wife of twenty-nine years was dead now for a year and a half. "I've finally been able to stop, and maybe I'm getting to the place I should have been a year ago." He was at his first counseling session and began to share his story.

"You know, when I was a kid I used run on the track team. I was a real jitterbug, always on the go. But I didn't know anything about running until Mary died. It was like I was running for my life. Or maybe running *from* my life. I couldn't stand the feelings.

"It was like everything—everything I knew—had fallen apart. I didn't know who I was anymore. I felt like I was going crazy. And if I weren't busy every minute I'd get panicky. As soon as any feelings—any feelings at all—started coming up I was gone. I couldn't stand it, and couldn't explain it. I just knew I was losing it and felt totally out of control.

"So I worked. And jogged. I don't even remember what all I did, but I felt like I didn't know what else to do. I know now I was kidding myself, thinking I was doing fine, but somewhere deep down I knew it was gaining on me. I knew I had to stop sometime, I was exhausted." Jim's head dropped to his chest as a lone tear gave witness to his sadness. The counseling room was quiet.

Slowly he began talking through his tears. "Now it's like somehow Mary has been waiting for me to get here. She's still with me—I can feel it—but I miss her so much I don't think I can stand it. It's like she's left me a huge boulder inside, an ache that's heavier than anything I've ever carried before. I don't know what to do."

Only months later did Jim recognize that his recognition of the pain was his first step in healing the pain he'd been holding. Now he wanted to tell his story, to spell out what he'd come to experience.

"I kept thinking I could get away from it, and I found out that I had to plow right into it, right through the middle of it. I'd been working more than I'd ever worked before. I volunteered for everything that came along. I partied, dated, kept thinking maybe if I met somebody else she would take my mind off Mary. The women I met and dated never knew I was expecting something from them I could only do for myself. I even resented Mary for dying and leaving me like I was. She knew I couldn't handle it. She should have taken better care of herself. But then neither of us was very good at that. So maybe it was my fault too that she got sick. We had no idea her heart was bad.

"Then I really felt sorry for myself. Nobody was as unlucky as I was. I knew God was down on me. I hadn't been the greatest guy, but I figured I hadn't been that bad. But then I figured that I must have deserved it or this all wouldn't have been happening. I went on that way as long as I could. Feeling terrible, in pain, running inside and out.

"That's when I fell apart. I got so miserable I gave in to it. I felt weak and helpless, but didn't know what else to do. Only now I know that it probably was the best thing and the only thing that could have turned me around. I never realized I could feel so bad and survive it.

"I guess I always believed that giving in to something like this was weak, that it meant I couldn't handle it. I thought I was supposed to be strong, and avoid anything that showed I wasn't as tough as I'd been brought up to be. Now I'm feeling like maybe facing it takes more toughness than avoiding it. Maybe that's the biggest lesson for me. Fighting the sadness and the pain, trying to get away from it, took more work and turned out to be like fighting some kind of battle I had no hope of winning that way.

"So here I am. Still sad, but a bit better now. I finally just said, 'Okay, you win, I miss her so much I can't stand it, but I can't stand fighting that feeling anymore either. So even if I crumble, I'm just going to let it happen.' And I gave up the fight. Only then did I come to know that the answer was there waiting for me."

WHEN WE MUST DEAL WITH PROBLEMS, WE INSTINCTIVELY REFUSE TO TRY THE WAY THAT LEADS THROUGH DARKNESS AND OBSCURITY. WE WISH ONLY TO HEAR OF UNEQUIVOCAL RESULTS, AND COMPLETELY FORGET THAT THESE RESULTS CAN ONLY BE BROUGHT ABOUT WHEN WE HAVE VENTURED INTO AND EMERGED AGAIN FROM THE DARKNESS.

Carl Jung

No! No! No!

Jenny's screams in the waiting room ricocheted like gunfire down the length of the hallway. Her dark eyes burned with shock and disbelief. Susan stood with Dr. Gilligan in stunned, uncomfortable silence, frozen in a moment of horrible truth. Then Susan reached out her arms to the young mother, and Jenny crumpled into a ball of sobs, shaking down to her toes.

Susan dreaded these times, even after many years as a nurse on the children's oncology floor. She knew that life changed the moment a feared diagnosis was confirmed. It would never again be the same. Once cancer entered a family's life, the foundation of that family's world was as shaken as if a major earthquake had shattered the ground beneath it. The stories parents told her through the years described that moment when the news was given as a stab in the heart that marked them forever. Though a mother herself, Susan could do no more than imagine the pain and grief and disbelief that this mother of a child with cancer felt. She ached with her own helplessness to heal things.

Over the next several months Susan was there each time Jenny brought Micah in for treatment. They went through the misery of chemotherapy together when Micah lost his hair, had terrible sores in his mouth, threw up all the time, and cried through every treatment while he clung to Jenny. Watching what had been a strong, growing seven-year-old lose his strength and color, become bloated with the medication and bruised from all the shots, Susan sometimes wondered how long she'd be able to keep working with children who faced death.

Jenny was a loving mom, fighting in whatever way she knew how, hoping against all hope that the cancer would lose its hold on her precious child. She vowed never to give up the fight. That fighting energy sustained them all through the early months of Micah's treatment. "We're gonna beat this" was Jenny's motto. She looked everywhere for help, questioning other parents about what worked for them, reading everything she could get her hands on about children and cancer, and straining with sheer willpower to make things different. She fought with the doctors and with family members when they began suggesting that it was time to ease up, to let go of trying so hard. At first Jenny saw them as traitors, as losing interest in Micah's healing. She felt angry with the lot of them and redoubled her struggles.

One day when Micah was in the hospital, Jenny hesitated at the door to his room. In his weakened, soft voice, he was talking to someone she couldn't see. "I can't come yet," she heard him say, "Mama's too sad. I have to stay with her till she's better."

Jenny pushed the door a bit farther to see who else was in the room with him and stopped quickly in disbelief. No one was there. Micah—not seeing her arrival—was still talking earnestly to someone only he could see. "Will you help her? Will you tell her it's okay?"

"Micah," Jenny reached out to him, moving quickly toward the bed. "Who are you talking to?"

"Oh, Mama, this is my guardian angel. She talks to me lots of times, mostly when nobody's here. I really like her."

Jenny's eyes scanned the room, seeing no one except her precious child, his face as bright as she'd ever seen it. He looked peaceful despite the hollow eyes and shrunken body. "Micah, what does she want with you?" Jenny felt fear rising in her chest.

"She says it's okay for me to come with her. She says I don't have to hurt much longer. She told me that God wants me to come."

"Micah," Jenny whispered, nearly holding her breath, "Do you want to go?"

"As soon as you tell me it's okay, Mama. I don't want you to be sad or mad anymore."

When Susan came into Micah's room fifteen minutes later, she found Jenny stretched out on the bed, her body as close as she could get to her little son—her arms holding him gently. Micah was sleeping peacefully, snuggled in his mother's arms. It was the beginning of Micah's gentle passage from this world.

Later Jenny told Susan that Micah showed her that it was time to stop fighting. She had done everything she knew how. She would have given her life for him if that could have changed the picture. She regretted none of her efforts. Only now she knew that the best she could give him and herself was the gift of letting be what was.

Micah was on his own journey through this world, his own path. Even though she was his mother, she couldn't control that path. She had given him life, had given him love and care and everything she knew how in this world, and now it was time to give him the freedom of his death. Her anger and resistance—so helpful earlier in Micah's illness—gave way to enormous sadness as Jenny allowed herself to let the experience be, to feel all its pain, sorrow, and emptiness, and to trust that she would make her way through.

NOTHING CAN MAKE UP FOR THE ABSENCE OF SOMEONE WHOM WE LOVE, AND IT WOULD BE WRONG TO TRY TO FIND A SUBSTITUTE; WE MUST SIMPLY HOLD OUT AND SEE IT THROUGH. THAT SOUNDS VERY HARD AT FIRST, BUT AT THE SAME TIME IT IS A GREAT CONSOLATION,

FOR THE GAP, AS LONG AS IT REMAINS UNFILLED, PRESERVES THE BONDS BETWEEN US. IT IS NONSENSE TO SAY THAT GOD FILLS THE GAP; GOD DOESN'T FILL IT, BUT ON THE CONTRARY, KEEPS IT EMPTY AND SO HELPS US TO KEEP ALIVE OUR FORMER COMMUNION WITH EACH OTHER, EVEN AT THE COST OF PAIN.

Dietrich Bonhoeffer

2

Openly Acknowledge What Has Been Lost

WHEN WE EXPERIENCE A LOSS, A HOLE OPENS UP INSIDE OF US. IT IS ALMOST AS IF THE LOSS ITSELF PLOWS RIGHT THROUGH US, LEAVING US GASPING FOR AIR. WE BLEED THROUGH THAT OPENING, AND SOMETIMES OLD WOUNDS ARE REOPENED. THINGS WE THOUGHT WERE SAFELY INSIDE, PATCHED OVER, HEALED, PROVE PAINFUL AGAIN IN THE WAKE OF THE NEW PAIN.

Rabbi David Wolpe

Grieving is hard work and highly stressful. Because it is so painful and asks so much of us, in the early days after a loss our whole being puts enormous effort into making it all go away. We want to wake up and find out we've only had a bad dream. Yet, despite all our efforts to avoid the painful truth—that something or someone significant is no longer here—the reality of it gradually begins nudging its way into our awareness. The natural numbness that has protected us from being overwhelmed starts to lift, and we come face to face with the empty place in our heart.

Take the case of Jane. Her husband had died several months before she came for counseling. "I think I'm getting worse," she began. "I thought I was doing pretty well, and now it feels worse than ever." Typically, when the unreality of loss begins to lift, the full impact of who or what we've lost emerges. The protection our minds give us in the early days of the loss begins to withdraw as we become more able to cope with the truth. This is when we describe our feelings as "getting worse."

Our healing is tied to admitting or acknowledging our loss. This process may move slowly or quickly. When the loss was unexpected, it takes us more time to finally come to believe it. When we've known that the loss was coming—perhaps even talked about it or cared for the person who was dying—we come more quickly to accept the truth of it.

We can help ourselves along in this process by thinking and talking about our loss. Remembering and reminiscing are part of what helps the loss become real to us. This is difficult in a society that more often or not wants to avoid anything painful and encourages us to avoid thinking or talking about unpleasant topics. We hear words like, "You've got to move on," or "Don't spend so much time feeling sorry for yourself. Just pick yourself up and get going again." This kind of advice often pushes us to pretend that nothing big has happened in our lives. And because openly grieving is so painful for us, sometimes we want to go along with the pretense. Almost everything in us wants things to be as they were before.

When we allow ourselves to talk about our grief, naming who and what we've lost, we may find out that our whole world has changed, that what we've known as life exists no longer. As we look more closely we realize that our world really *has* changed. It will no longer be as it was before.

We also will find changes in ourselves, especially in our new set of circumstances. We might be overwhelmed with this "new me." We feel like a different person. As we look more closely at what we've lost, we find a whole array of losses that are attached to the one major loss. "I miss talking with her about work," Jim said. "She had a great sense of what I was doing and I could bounce things off her whenever I was in a jam. Nobody else can do that as well. Besides, she had the craziest sense of humor of anybody I know. I miss that."

When someone dear to us dies, we not only lose that person, we also lose all the things we associated with that dear one's presence: her companionship, her support, and her personal interest in us. Even when there are others remaining who mean a lot to us, no one else in our world is quite like this one important person. Other losses—jobs, possessions, dreams, or hopes—also will change our lives. So we may have lost a sense of the future.

Naming and owning the losses builds the groundwork that supports our grieving in a healthy way. Avoiding the whole truth, putting aside how huge its implications are in our lives and how much we are being asked to change, or refusing to even think about the loss seem to be ways of trying to hold on, when all of life is asking us to let go. Until we can come to see and own up to the fact that our lives will be powerfully affected by our losses, we can't begin to move through the losses to new life. Our lives are on hold while we are trying to live in a way that no longer exists for us.

Though admitting the fact of our loss may be more painful than we think we can bear, saying the words, naming the loss—to ourselves and to others—are important steps on our journey toward healing. Our goal is never to forget the person or whatever else has moved out of our lives. Our goal is to begin adapting our lives to new circumstances. Though our steps may be faltering and filled with sadness, we are walking the path that leads us toward wholeness and healing.

AND ONE OF THE PARADOXES OF THIS WORK IS THAT WE COME TO KNOW OUR GRIEFS AS OUR MOST PRECIOUS POSSESSIONS. THE VERY THINGS WE WISH TO AVOID, REJECT OR FLEE FROM TURN OUT TO BE THE *PRIMA MATERIA* FROM WHICH ALL REAL GROWTH COMES.

Andrew Harvey
and Mark Matousek

Openly Acknowledge What Has Been Lost

- On paper, write the who, what, when, where, and how of a recent loss. Pour out everything. No matter how hard it is to face them, know that healing begins with naming your losses and recognizing their importance in your life.

- Repeat this affirmation several times each day until its message becomes clear and helpful: "I will walk through my losses rather than try to walk around them. I will open my arms to them, seeking the blessings they might hold for me."

• Sit with your sadness and loss. Recognize all the ways in which your major loss has brought other losses in its wake. Write down the major and lesser losses if helpful. By writing them down, you can return to them, add to them as new thoughts arise, and pray with them when any one of them asks for particular attention.

TO SUPPRESS FEELING IS TO DEPRIVE KNOWLEDGE OF ITS POINT. TO BE AFRAID OF FEELINGS IS TO BE AFRAID OF FINALITIES, OF EVER GETTING ANYWHERE.

Robert Johann

Charade

I got up at the same time as always. I showered, shaved, and dressed for "work." A quick breakfast was next, and I was off as usual, pulling out of the driveway just about the time the school bus came to gather up the kids.

"See you tonight," I'd call out at Margie as I headed out toward the freeway, a trip I'd made so many times I didn't even have to think about it. At first it was easy. Everything seemed so natural. In fact, that's what was keeping me going, doing the same routine I'd always done. I'd just drive into town and wander around all day, almost in a daze, till it was time to go home. Then I'd make up stories about what had happened all day at work.

Margie had no idea my job didn't exist anymore. There was no way I could tell her. I had walked into the meeting my boss called two weeks earlier, never dreaming my life was about to nosedive. My job was everything to me. I'd climbed the company ladder like everybody dreams of doing. Sure, I'd seen many co-workers being laid off. I just never dreamed it would happen to me. I thought I was pretty important. My salary was great. The thought they'd let me go never entered my mind.

I found out that fateful day that it's not only the grassroots people that get canned. I should have known that saving a salary like mine would be a coup. (We were forever looking for ways to cut costs.) Hell, I was the one who used to figure out which other people we could get rid of. Still, I never thought it would be me.

How was I supposed to face my family and friends? I felt like a failure. I was so mad I wanted to see those who fired me lose their precious jobs too. "Let them see what it feels like," I'd think to myself. I'd gotten so much respect because of my position, but now I felt that respect stripped away.

I kept on the lookout when I went into town every day. I sure didn't want to run into anybody I knew who was going to ask me what or how I was doing. I had no idea what I'd say. I knew what they'd think, "Poor sucker. Thought he was really somebody. Now he's a nobody."

The hardest thing for me was Margie and the kids. It always felt good—I knew Margie was proud of me— to be able to say "Get whatever you need, I'm making good money." That's what a guy who's worth anything wants to be able to say. They didn't have a clue what had happened. I felt like such a loser. The company gave me some severance pay, but that would only last so long. We haven't saved much with the kids in school and buying so many things they needed.

My severance had almost run out before I could tell her what had happened. I must have been showing my problems in some way though because one day she asked me point blank what was wrong. I couldn't just tell her it had been a bad day. It was getting too weird, going off everyday and living a lie. I knew that was no way to live and that my choices were to keep the charade up or to come clean and tell her about it.

I put off telling Margie. Then one morning, I just couldn't pull myself out of bed. I almost felt paralyzed. It scared me to the point that I just broke down. I cried like a baby. Everything came pouring out, and I almost couldn't stop. Thank God I've got the wife I have. She told me she knew something was wrong but didn't know how to ask me. She was so glad when I told her, even though she was really upset, too, about how I had felt the need to hide it from her.

We wound up talking for a long time about all the things I was feeling. It was hard to do it but I was so glad that finally I could tell her about losing my job. I almost felt like I was going crazy. I was really afraid I'd lose her and the kids, too. Marge had a hard time dealing with my job loss too. She wanted to know exactly what happened. Once I poured it all out and we cried together, we started talking about what to do now.

We still haven't worked it out. Margie was angry at the company, but angry with me too. I think now she sees that it really wasn't my fault in any way. I should have told her when it happened. But we're talking now. That helps a lot. When I was keeping it all inside, I really felt awful.

I know lots of people lose a job. Some get through it and some stay angry forever, it seems. I don't want to do that. I've still got myself, Margie and the kids, and God, and I know I can do lots of things. I just have to get myself going now and try a new job. Who knows, things may end up better than they ever were. We'll see.

EXAMINE ME, GOD, AND KNOW MY
MIND; TEST ME, AND UNDERSTAND
MY ANXIOUS THOUGHTS. WATCH
LEST I FOLLOW ANY PATH THAT
GRIEVES YOU; LEAD ME IN THE EVER-
LASTING WAY.

Psalm 139

If I Don't See Him, I Won't Suffer

I still don't know just why it was so important for me to be part of Jeremy's life, but I know I was there for a reason. Actually, I only knew of Jeremy at the very beginning and the very end of his life. But he touched me deeply all the same.

Jeremy was born to parents who wanted him so much they could hardly wait for his arrival. When Martha and Steve found out she was pregnant both of their families threw a party. Tiny clothes, toys, blankets, and gifts flooded into the household. A room was painted and carpeted, decorated with love and hope in colors that would welcome a baby girl or boy. Like so many other expectant parents, Martha and Steve just wanted a beautiful, healthy baby.

Somewhere during the middle months of her pregnancy Martha knew that something was amiss. It wasn't confirmed for a while, but as the baby's birth came closer and closer Martha and Steve's fear and concern grew. They prayed, cried, and worried about the baby. And they waited. Tests confirmed that there was difficulty: their precious and long-awaited baby had serious physical problems. Some worry even surrounded the baby's ability to survive birth.

After birth by Cesarean section, the tiny one was whisked away for examination and care. Martha didn't see him. The operating room was quiet, without its usual lusty cry, announcement, congratulations, and tears of joy. The doctor simply said, "You have a little boy." Martha remembered that Steve's face was white and that a look of horrible pain crossed his face as he glanced at the baby.

I knew none of this until later. As a counselor at the hospital, I frequently was part of painful and difficult experiences. The beginning of Jeremy's life, however, didn't include me until two days later. The call from the maternity ward came early in the afternoon, on a bright, warm day. As the story was unfolded to me, my heart ached for this young mom and dad.

"This baby was born with several severe physical abnormalities," the nurse said, explaining their seriousness to me. "The dad has seen him and talked with the doctors, and the plan is that there is no way they can take him home. Dad decided that his wife shouldn't even see the baby. He thought it would be too hard on her. Arrangements have been made to place the newborn in a facility where he can be cared for. The parents are set to go home today."

"Well, things have now changed. Mom says there's no way she'll leave here without seeing her baby. She's crying. Her husband's trying to get her to just come home. He doesn't want her to be hurt anymore. But she's saying that as the time got closer for her to go home, she knew she couldn't leave until she saw her child. No one knows what to do for her. It'll be really hard for her to see him. Can you come and help us and maybe talk with her?"

By the time I got to her room, Martha had become even more adamant in her resolve to see the baby. "He's mine and nobody is going to keep me from him," her voice was strong and clear. I told her that I had no intention of trying to talk her out of her wishes. I certainly understood her husband's effort to protect her as well as her own ache to see her baby. I also believed she, like most humans, have an enormous ability to handle what comes into our lives. The question for me was how to help her, how to support her in what was obviously a very painful experience. She told me her story, and we discussed the problems her son had. And then she and I went to meet Jeremy.

As we walked through the newborn intensive care unit, past nine or ten other tiny beings beginning life with a struggle, I prayed for support for Martha and for guidance. I'll never forget this new mom's touchingly heartfelt greeting to her little misshapen child. "Oh, my baby!" she wept as she gently touched him. And then, after a few minutes of silence when she took in his whole appearance, she whispered to me, "Joan, look how beautiful his little hands and feet are! He's got all his fingers and toes!"

Several days later Jeremy went home with his mom and dad. Home Care nurses came in regularly and helped them set up a plan of care. I wasn't to hear from them again until nine years later. Those nine years weren't always easy—marked both by struggle and delight—but became an experience of life they would never regret.

I was leading a retreat for grieving folks, and thought a younger and older woman who had come in late together looked vaguely familiar. I discovered they were grieving the death of their son and grandson, which had happened only two weeks before. Grandma got out a picture to show me a somewhat misshapen nine-year-old at a birthday party. "What a gift he was," Grandma said. "He brought joy to the whole family."

"What was his name?" I asked the mom.
"Jeremy," she said.

BLESSED ARE THOSE WHO MOURN,
THEY SHALL BE COMFORTED.

Gospel of Matthew

3

Be Aware That Your Loss Is Like No Other

NO SITUATION IN LIFE IS EXACTLY
LIKE ANOTHER. BESIDES THE FACT
THAT SITUATIONS DIFFER——WHO
HAS DIED, WHEN AND WHERE THEY
DIED——THE IMPORTANT FACT
REMAINS THAT EACH PERSON IS A
UNIQUE HUMAN BEING EXPRESSING
A UNIQUE PERSONALITY. . . . THUS,
ALL ASPECTS OF AN INDIVIDUAL'S
LIFE WILL HAVE A BEARING ON THE
WAY THE PERSON DEALS WITH
GRIEF.

Catherine Sanders

E very loss has its own signature. Though the entire universe operates in cycles of life to death to life, over and over again, and we each live through so many of the same kinds of losses through the course of our lives, we experience each one in our own individual way. We tend to follow the same basic pattern of grieving as others do, but our experiences will always be stamped with our unique imprint. Each loss reflects the relationships and connections we make, and the meanings and values we attach to every person and to everything in our lives.

Our losses come at particular times in our lives—when we're in good health or ill, when things are going smoothly or are otherwise difficult, when we have good friends around us or no one to turn to. All of these circumstances contribute to the way we make our way through our losses. Losses never come in a vacuum, but always in the context of the rest of our lives.

I have often spoken with widows in support groups. While these women will talk of many similar experiences, each one knows that her loss is different from the loss of the others. Each one says that her husband and she were like no other couple. Each one came to this time in her journey when a whole set of unique circumstances surrounded her besides the death of a spouse.

When we started life we had little idea about the meanings of particular connections or relationships. We think we just are. We tend to live our lives with a sense of ourselves as wholly apart from others, even though we relate to them in many ways. We often have little awareness of how intricately intertwined we all are or of the role others play in our own sense of wholeness.

All too often, only when we lose something or someone important do we wake up to how much we're connected. Then we know that each of our relationships tells us something about who we are. Our sense of ourselves comes through all the connections we make to people and ideas, to jobs and roles, and to likes and dislikes.

We learn nuances of behavior and thought from significant people and incorporate these into our character.

We play a similar role helping to shape the character of others. Because of the uniqueness of both persons in any relationship, the relationship itself becomes unique. When an important person dies or leaves us as in divorce or separation, when our dreams don't come true, when a job is taken away or we retire, when a precious pet dies or runs away, when we find our eyes squinting to see in the distance or our ears straining to hear what's being said, and in all the ways we age, we lose a vital part of ourselves. Only we know the importance of what we lose. And sometimes it takes us a long while to realize what something we lost really meant to us.

In fact, many times we have no idea how important something is to us until we lose it. It is in times like these that we hear ourselves saying things like, "I feel like there's a big empty spot in my world." Or, as one man said after the death of his wife, "It's like somebody took my life and tore it up in little pieces and threw it up in the air. And I have no idea how it's all going to come back together again."

Sometimes when we look at another person's life, we think we know how the other person feels. But from the outside, losses that seem big may not be what we imagine. And what may not look terribly big in looking at another person's situation, may be huge in that person's consciousness. We can never know what a loss means to another person unless that person tells us. So it may take us a while to begin to see how important something or someone was to us.

After any loss, we may need to ask ourselves just what we're grieving. What we grieve for is not only the presence of the person who died or whose love we lost, or the job that was so important to us, but the unique relationship that was there. Whomever or whatever we lost, we need to ask:

- What did that person, job, or thing mean to me?

- What importance or significance had I given that person in my life?

We might see that this particular person is the only one who shared our interest in something important to us. Perhaps this person was the only one who understood or who supported us when we chose a certain path for our lives. Maybe the job we lost gave us the prestige we'd been looking for or the sense of accomplishment we couldn't quite explain.

I have often seen this played out in families. When a mother or father dies, each child, no matter the age, will have had a relationship with that parent dissimilar to anyone else's relationship. All the children will be sad and grieve the death of the parent, but each one will be grieving what that parent meant to him or her, whether they had a loving, supportive relationship, or whether the relationship was distant and indifferent.

"I knew I was my dad's favorite," Tim told me one day. "He always said he loved us all the same, but my brother and I knew I could get away with things he never could." We were talking about the death of Tim's dad, and how he felt sorry for his brother Steve. "Steve always wanted to feel special to Dad, and kept hoping that would happen. It never did. He was always trying to do things to make Dad proud of him, and now he feels like he was wasting his time." Clearly, Steve and Tim would grieve their father's death differently.

So while the process of grieving can have many common features, there will always be distinctive characteristics in every experience of loss. We each can see that the signature of our own losses will be uniquely tailored. We grieve most healthily and well when we recognize the uniqueness of our own loss and let it be our guide.

Everything that happens to you
is your teacher. The secret is to
sit at the feet of your own life

AND BE TAUGHT BY IT. . . . THE FIRST
STEP IN FINDING YOUR WAY SOME-
WHERE IS TO DISCOVER WHERE YOU
ARE TO BEGIN WITH.

Polly Berrien Berends

Be Aware That Your Loss Is Like No Other

- Think about the journey of your own life and name how particular lost persons or objects were important to you. What place did each have in your life? Did this person (or whatever you lost) give you a sense of purpose or value? Did it contribute to or break down your sense of confidence? Name the unique aspect of each loss.

- Think about how much you are like others in your grief. Also, what are the ways each loss in your life stands out differently from others? Can you accept your differences?

- Consider your own life story and know that it points out for you the direction of your grief. When you come to see the particular ways the person or thing you lost was important, then you know what needs attention or focus. For example, as you examine your losses, you may own up to having had a troubled relationship with the one who died. This may make your grieving more difficult or at least different than it would have been had the relationship been smooth. You may need to deal more directly with your guilt, anger, or sadness about what might have been.

- If you were in a troubled relationship with someone who has died, write a letter to that person now. Talk about your true feelings, the good times and the difficult ones. Several letters of this type may need to be written to work through your feelings. When you have reached a place of serenity, perform a ritual burning of these letters. As the paper turns to smoke and ashes, let go of your troubled feelings and invite peace into your heart.

• Affirm the reality of your situation, whether you like it or not. Choose to deal with life as it presents itself to you, even the aspects you wish were not so. Begin by identifying each loss and then claiming it as your own.

• Loss happens not only with death, but also in a wide variety of other situations we face. Though you may not think of them as losses, many experiences may ask you to grieve. Examine the ways—other than death—that you are being asked now to let go of something or someone important.

• If you are actively grieving the loss of someone or something important right now, how did that person, job, or experience say something about who you are?

I'VE BEEN WITH MANY PEOPLE WHOSE GRIEF HAS BEEN BEYOND BEARING. AND IN SOME WAYS IT HAS BEEN THE BEST THING THAT EVER HAPPENED TO THEM. FOR THEY COME TO PLUMB THE DEPTHS OF THEIR BEING.

Stephen Levine

Complicated Grief

A mid-afternoon break in my workshop on grieving and loss offered a moment of respite. Participants began milling around, chatting with each other, or wandering off for fresh air. As usual a few folks came up to comment or ask a question they hesitated to ask before the whole group. I could see one woman in a state of indecision, apparently wondering whether to come with her question or not. As others began to move off after brief conversations, she stood back until the very end, then came up tentatively like she knew that if she didn't speak up now she never would. She blurted out the question that was bothering her.

"Can I tell you that it was a real relief when my husband died?"

A flavor of both challenge and guilt tinged the edges of the question.

"You can tell me anything you want," I said, waiting to see if there was more.

For a moment she was quiet, and then as tears welled up in her eyes she whispered, "I've never said that out loud before. I hope it's okay that I said it. People are always giving me their sympathy, and I just say 'Thank you,' I never tell them how hard it all was."

Though I never did learn her name, the pain she carried touched me. Once she opened the door to her personal sadness and loss, the whole story came flooding out. It was obvious she'd been waiting a long time, looking for a place to be able to speak it to someone.

"My husband was an awful man," she began. "No, wait. Not always. When we first got together he was fine, though I have to keep reminding myself of those times. If I had known then what would happen later, I would have run so fast no one could have caught me. But after some of our kids were born he started to drink hard. First it was off and on, and then it was all the time. I should have left him then.

"I didn't think it could get worse, but it did. We had more kids and that didn't make it any easier. We were screaming at each other all the time. I was exhausted and mad, and didn't know what to do. Sometimes he'd work and sometimes not. He'd just lie around the house doing nothing. I wound up trying to work for a while to get some money, but the kids would be home with him, and he'd start picking on them. My family didn't know the half of it. When I did say something to my mother she told me I made my bed, so now I had to lie in it.

"Then he started beating me. And when the kids would try to stop him he'd turn on them. I thought so many times of leaving, but I didn't know where to go, and didn't know anybody that would take in me and all my kids. I got really afraid of him. One time when I said I wanted to leave, he told me he'd find me and kill me if I ever tried it. I even thought about killing myself, but I knew things would be worse for my kids. They needed me. So I kept praying that things would change, but they never did.

"Gradually I could tell he wasn't feeling good, and then I knew he was really sick. I had to take him to the doctor sometimes, and he was in a lot of pain. The doctor said there wasn't anything he could do. He told my husband and me that his liver was damaged from all the drink. He could only give him some medicine to help with the pain. He got mad at the doctor, said he didn't know what he was talking about, and had me take him to another one. The same story. This all made him really mad, and he thought I'd put the doctors up to it.

"Well, little by little he got worse and worse, until he had to go to the hospital and stay. He only lasted a few days and then he died.

"I can only tell you it was like somebody took a millstone from around my neck. I could never describe the feeling of relief. But then I get to feeling guilty about that. It's been a while but I still find myself looking over my shoulder at times, afraid he's there or will show up. When it hits me that he's gone, the relief floods all over me. It's like I can breathe again.

"But then sometimes I start feeling sad about him, and about me and what our life turned into. I think of all the missed opportunities we had for having a good life, for the kids and us. I still feel mad at him for all that. I know some of the kids feel angry with him still. Life didn't have to be the way it was for us. I get mad at myself sometimes, too, for not knowing how to make it stop. There probably are some things I could have done. Maybe somebody could have helped us. I don't know, my feelings are just all mixed up.

"It seems such a shame to waste a life like that, his and mine. All that fighting and hurting each other. You'd think we would have been smarter than that. And I worry about the kids, and what all this will mean in their lives. I sure hope none of them follow his example. Actually, I hope none of them follow mine either. I should have figured out something that would have made life better. Now what I mostly have are memories I'd rather forget."

O GOD WHO LOVES RICH VARIETY, WHO CREATED NOT SIMPLY A SIN-GLE TREE, BUT TREES OF ALL KINDS, SIZES AND SHAPES, LET ME SEE THE VAST VARIETY IN WAYS OF MOURN-ING. GRANT ME THE GRACE NEVER TO JUDGE OTHERS IN HOW OR HOW LONG THEY GRIEVE.

Edward Hays

Home Sweet Home

L eaving the paved county road to drive into the mountains, my whole being told me I was coming into something special. Scrub oak, chokecherry bushes, and hawthorn trees hugged the edges of the dirt road and a few golden aspen peeked out like patches of sunlight from the dark evergreen. As we climbed, the view opened out until the whole of a great snow-capped peak stood like a sentinel over the valley below.

"Here we are," the realtor said as we turned onto a drive that could have been winding into a secret garden. I found myself silent as we climbed out of the car, not wanting to break the spell that seemed to envelop me since we'd turned off the pavement below. I felt like the little boy I once was, discovering a place that could be my very own. Everything fit. Even the house, built into the hillside with its arms open in welcome, drew me in. There was no question that this was home. This was the place I'd been looking for forever, and all nestled into enough land to give me the quiet and solitude I craved.

It was a wonderful find and the purchase went smoothly, as did the next ten years or so as I basked in what was for me the perfection of the place. I loved it just as it was and looked forward to the continuing gifts the setting gave me. As I lived in my "secret garden," however, I also lived in the real world. Other forces and other ideas were at work.

At the same time as I was delighting in my "perfect place" other homeowners in the area were seeing it as an entrepreneur's dream. Why not take this hillside and develop it? There was lots of money to be made. Simply subdivide the lots and more homes could be built.

Thoughts of fracturing the peace and solitude and integrity of the area by developing the land were horrifying to me. What I wanted from the place was totally opposite from what some neighbors wanted. But besides me a few others also loved the quietness and opposed the destruction of our homes. Luckily, a covenant that prevented such development had been in place for many years. We trusted that covenant.

When those in favor of development challenged the covenant, we hired our own lawyer to protect our purchases. The next few years were full of anxiety, anger, and distress—the very experiences we had sought to avoid in moving out of the turmoil of big cities into the quiet peace of the mountain valley. Neighbor was set against neighbor, secret meetings were held on both sides, and plans made for ensuring one's own wishes. A great deal of time was spent in worry.

After spending more money than we wanted to, we finally won our case in court. For a few years a semblance of peace was upon the area until an enterprising neighbor with a strong entrepreneurial bent hit upon a plan to divide the covenant. Through subtle threats he was also able to divide the neighbors until too few held to the old covenant. The fight was over. The land could be divided and developed.

I felt a huge loss. In my mind I saw so much of my little Eden crumbling. I couldn't believe that what was so precious to me could be taken away—my solitude, my quietness, the magnificence of the natural view— the externals that allowed and supported my way of life. It seemed unfair, and I was distressed.

Over a period of time, I mulled it over in my mind. Actually, it took up more worrying and stewing time than I wanted it to. But I began to come up with some positive factors in the decision. I no longer had to worry about a huge lawsuit, which I could ill afford. My own forestland protected much of my view. I didn't have to make any change to my own land. And the development rights were limited by county rules. I could still be as quiet and peaceful as I chose, though I had no idea what would be happening all around me.

What struck me over time was that there was nothing "wrong" with what the developers wanted. Nor was there anything "wrong" with what I wanted. They were different. We each have different values and connections in our lives. My grief came about because of my sense of losing what was precious to me. As they were probably also grieving when the decision had been made to stand by the covenant, over the loss of what was important to them.

So though I try to find the positives in the decision, I still regret it all and feel some sadness about it. Whatever development the future brings may have definite impact on my home setting. I don't like that idea at all. I don't know what kind of noise and traffic might be part of it, or who will want to build what. I'll have no control over all that. So while I plan to stay there and make the best of what I have in my beautiful spot, I know I'll still be grieving as I watch things change on my mountainside.

No person's grief or mourning response occurs in a vacuum. Rather it is influenced, shaped, and determined by a constellation of factors that combine to render a mourner's response unique—as individual as a fingerprint.

Therese A. Rando

4

Allow the Wide Range of Emotion That Comes With Grief

IN CHOOSING TO FACE THE NIGHT, I
TOOK MY FIRST STEPS TOWARD THE
SUNRISE.

Gerald L. Sittser

Our whole being is touched by our losses, not just our mind and heart. We can expect to be totally shaken and affected when we grieve. After working so hard to avoid the truth of a loss, the reality eventually will break through into our awareness. As we let our losses become more conscious in our lives, and allow ourselves to name and acknowledge our losses, emotion wells up in us and helps us express the pain of our wounding.

Our emotions are ways of expressing what's going on within us, and are also ways of communicating with others. "When I was feeling so low, and wanting to cry all the time, I found myself telling people I was fine," Joyce told me one day, "But sometimes my tears would start to flow, and I couldn't hold them back. They were more honest than my words. I was saying what I thought people wanted me to say, not how I really felt. I think my tears really helped me. They told the truth."

Despite what our society teaches us, emotions are not signs of weakness. So often during grief, people will describe themselves as "needing to be strong"— usually for someone else. What they likely mean is that they must hold their emotions in check. Sometimes when a particular responsibility demands our attention, we can put our emotions on the back burner for a short period of time. However, we create problems for ourselves when we don't give full attention to what we've put aside. Real strength is shown in the healthy expression of appropriate emotions.

Sometimes we're surprised at the emotions that arise. Many people have told me of their anger with a person close them who died. "She knew I'd have a terrible time without her," one elderly gentleman said about his wife. "We talked about it, and agreed that I should be the first one to go. And then she went and left me." Such anger arises as we experience our huge helplessness in the face of death and loss. So we look for someone to be responsible.

Sometimes a sense of relief, anger, or even our own ineptness may provoke guilt feelings. When a death has been a long time coming, when we've become emotionally exhausted at its approach, or when our caregiving has worn us out physically, relief may accompany the time of death. Before the long-coming death of her husband whom she dearly loved, Elizabeth burst out in sobs one day and said, "Why doesn't God take him? I don't know how much longer he can suffer, or I can go on!" And even before she took the next breath, she cried, "Oh, what am I saying? How could I even think such a thing?"

In grief we may become a battleground of conflicting emotions: sadness, anger, guilt, fear, doubt, despair, and other emotions we may not even be able to name. These might share the company of loneliness, worry, and even a sense of unreality.

Some emotions are deemed fine while others are judged not appropriate. Most of us have grown up hearing:

"Don't be angry."

"Don't cry."

"Don't feel bad."

Consequently, the only acceptable emotions we feel we can express are gratitude, joy, and happiness. The most common emotions in grief become the "enemy" that we struggle to overcome. So we wind up trying to fight off what we might truly feel, and substitute "being strong" for others.

Unexpressed emotions do not seem to disappear. Rather, they tend to go underground and affect us in other ways. Thus, we miss the wisdom of our emotions, the healing they can bring to our experience. Healthy grieving allows us to accept the emotions that arise, to name them, and to allow them to express our grief appropriately.

Interestingly, when we stop fighting our emotions and let them flow, the emotions seem to diminish. Fighting to stop an emotion has just the opposite effect: The emotion tends to escalate or goes underground and waits for another opportunity to be expressed.

Some of us are afraid to let our emotions flow for fear they will overwhelm us. I have often heard, "If I once start crying, I'm afraid I'll never be able to stop!" Some of us keep our emotions at bay "because they will hurt too much." Other mourners tell of their fear of "chasing other people off" with their emotions, also expressing the sentiment that "people have enough troubles of their own, they don't want to hear about mine." We've rarely been taught that meaningful and appropriate expression of emotion is healthy. And, most of the ways to express emotions are healthy. The only inappropriate expressions of our emotions are any destructive expression. Hurting another person or striking out at others isn't healthy for either side.

The expression of emotional pain often touches our very being and encourages us to reach out to another. From the depths of our own experience we have some common understanding of how much our grieving hurts and we can offer our love, understanding, and care to another person who is grieving.

WHEN EMOTIONS ARE EXPRESSED— WHICH IS TO SAY THAT THE BIOCHEM-ICALS THAT ARE THE SUBSTRATE OF EMOTION ARE FLOWING FREELY— ALL SYSTEMS ARE UNITED AND MADE WHOLE. WHEN EMOTIONS ARE REPRESSED, DENIED, NOT ALLOWED TO BE WHATEVER THEY MAY BE, OUR NETWORK PATHWAYS GET BLOCKED, STOPPING THE FLOW OF THE VITAL . . . UNIFYING CHEMICALS THAT RUN BOTH OUR BIOLOGY AND OUR BEHAVIOR.

Candace B. Pert

Allow the Wide Range of Emotion That Comes With Grief

- Instead of trying to avoid expressing emotion, turn your full attention to whatever you're feeling. See if you can name what the emotion is that is lurking.

- Simply let your emotion flow. Don't try to stop it. Just be with it. Don't judge it or decide that it should or shouldn't be there.

- As you sit quietly, thinking of the loss in your life, speak to whatever emotion arises. Welcome it and simply let it be. Ask it for its wisdom. Consider writing these dialogues, letting one part of them—their "strong side"—talk with another part, their profound sadness or anger or guilt.

- Sometimes when emotion is intense, certain thoughts come with it. Jot them in your journal. Go back to them on occasion for their lessons and gifts. What do they point to in your life that wants attention?

- Be aware when your words are in conflict with your emotions, when you tell others you are "fine" but your body tells you something different. What would it take to be more honest with your emotion? Are you willing to respect what it tells you?

- If music, especially music that you shared with the one who is gone, helps you get in touch with your feelings, listen attentively to the music. Allow whatever feelings come to flow freely.

- A famous psychologist once said that emotions are "vital signs" of life. Everyone has and feels emotion. Not everyone values the wisdom of his or her emotions. Do you allow your emotions to show that you are alive, or do you force them underground?

YOU WILL SURVIVE DESPITE YOUR PAIN. ALL FEELINGS ARE TRANSITORY AND WILL PASS.

Robert Miller

Three Red Roses

It was late when I made my last rounds of the evening shift, ten o'clock or so. Corridors were dark on most of the hospital floors, and the nurses were buzzing around quietly finishing up the treatments and medications of the shift, settling patients down for the night.

Though it was always busy, I loved the evening shift. All of the visitors, activities, and other distractions of daytime seemed to back off then, and what felt like the "realness" of the vulnerable people who were patients came creeping out of their protective daytime hiding places. These were the hours, as it got dark, when folks would talk about their worries and fears, sometimes cry a bit, reminisce, and struggle with the "why's" of life. I always felt privileged to share those times.

However, on this particular evening I was tired, eager to finish my rounds, give my report to the night supervisor, and be off to bed. Rounding the corner from the elevator and approaching the nursing station on East 200, I almost crashed into a middle-aged man with a little girl in tow. She looked to be early school age, six or seven, and visiting hours had been over for more than an hour.

"Excuse me, sir. Did you have permission to bring the little girl in now?" I asked politely and matter-of-factly.

I was totally unprepared for his reaction. As if speaking through a megaphone, he started a tirade. "Who do you think you are," he shouted at me. "There's no way you're going to keep me out. This is the worst hospital I've ever had anything to do with. Nobody here knows what they're doing, and nobody cares about people who are sick. The way you treat people here is terrible. I'd never come back in a million years the way things are here."

Heat emanated from this man's words, expression, and his menacing, challenging stance. It felt like someone had opened a blast furnace, and I was standing too close. Instinctively I took a step back. The tirade continued, and I don't even remember all he said, except that it was searing, furious. Needless to say, I felt overpowered by his anger, and even a bit frightened.

Somehow, though, I was able to remain silent, not to argue. The thought crossed my mind that I had no idea what his story was, and that there must be something terribly wrong. Trying to be rational at this point, even though I too was feeling under attack and emotional, would make no connection with his distress. I simply stood with him. Glancing into the nursing station I could see the wide eyes and shocked expressions of two nurses.

Before I could come up with anything to say, this furious man finished his tirade with a final salvo and shouted directly in my face, "You are the most cruel and unkind person I have ever met!" He pushed me aside, took his child's hand, and continued down the darkened hallway.

Needless to say, the nurses were as unnerved as I was. "Who was that?" I asked, and was told it was the husband of a patient who was quite ill. In fact, she probably would not be able to return home.

"But we've never seen him act like that," they said. "He's usually fine. He doesn't say much to us, but we've never seen anything like this from him. And we've never seen the little girl. I guess she's their child." We decided not to interfere with his visit that evening.

Shortly after coming on duty the following afternoon, I was paged to the information desk in the lobby. Much to my huge surprise, there stood the man of the great anger waiting for me, three red roses in his hand. "Do you have a few minutes so I can talk with you?" he asked quietly. "I want to explain about last evening." And then he handed me the roses.

His story touched my heart. He and his wife had come to their marriage late, each in their forties, never married before. They never expected a child at their ages, and "lo and behold along came our little one who's been a wonderful gift." He described a beautiful relationship, a marriage and family that basically got along, made its way through whatever difficulties came up, and was a real sharing of love.

Then he told of his wife's illness, of coming in for tests, and finding cancer. He told of hope that the cancer could be cured and that they could be a family again. "We had decided not to tell our daughter just how sick her mother is, since she'd be coming home soon. She had never been to the hospital to see her. We just thought it best to wait a few more days 'til she came home." His voice began to tremble and his eyes filled with tears.

"Yesterday the doctor called me and said we had to talk. I went to his office at 1:30, and he told me the whole picture had changed. The cancer was getting worse. They had discussed her case at some meeting, and decided that no treatment would help. And then he said, 'She probably won't get home like we planned, so you better go home and tell your daughter.'

"I don't know where I went when I left his office. I walked and walked. I was in a daze. I couldn't believe what he said. It couldn't be true. I must have spent several hours just roaming around in a fog. I guess it was the beginning twilight that sort of woke me up, and I knew Katie would be waiting for me to fix supper at home. It took me a while to find my car.

"All the way home I kept going over and over in my mind how to tell her. How do you tell a seven-year-old that she's going to lose the most important person in the world?" By this time he was openly crying without embarrassment, tears rolling down his cheeks.

"When I walked in the front door, Katie was waiting for me. She knew something was wrong because I was so late. Before I could say anything, she said to me, 'Daddy, Mommy's going to die, isn't she?' I didn't know what to say. I felt lost for words.

"We sat down in my big chair, and I held her, and for a long time we cried and cried and cried. And then we started talking about Mommy, and how much we love her, and how we didn't want her to die, and how we didn't know what we were going to do without her.

"Then, somewhere around nine o'clock or so, when we'd gotten a little quieter, Katie said to me, 'Daddy, will you take me to the hospital now to see Mommy?' And I said, 'Sure.' And we came. That's when we ran into you."

HOW ELSE BUT THROUGH A

BROKEN HEART

MAY LORD CHRIST ENTER IN.

Oscar Wilde

Letting Go

An older woman whom I had known casually for years called and asked me if I'd come over and "talk a little bit." I found her in her kitchen. She poured me a cup of tea and I sat down at the table and listened to her story.

"I've known the time was coming close," she began. "I've known it for quite a while, but never would I let anybody else know that I knew. I couldn't bear it. In front of my kids and everybody, I act like things could go on this way forever.

"I know if I say something to any one of them, they'll start putting pressure on. I can't do it that way. I have to do it in my own time, or I can't do it. Besides, not one of my kids knows what it's like to be me, to be my age and be coming to the place where you know you have to start relinquishing your whole life. At least that's what it feels like. And really, that's what it is."

She was puttering around her kitchen, talking more to herself than she was talking to me. I sat with my hands around a cup of her peppermint tea keeping warm. I had an inkling that this was what it would be about. Her children were worried about her living alone in the big old house they'd grown up in. They'd been arguing among themselves about who should talk with her about this. Every time any of them even came close to the idea of her getting more care, giving up the old house, coming to live with one of them, or even going to a nursing home, they'd meet her steely side. There'd be no more conversation in that direction.

One day, her oldest son put a newspaper clipping on her kitchen counter so she'd see it. He didn't dare give it to her himself. The article was about older drivers and the importance of regular evaluation and testing to be sure they were still competent on the road. It told of several accidents that involved drivers over seventy-five and included questions about when one should consider giving up a driver's license. Her sons and daughter had been worrying about her driving for a while.

She hit the ceiling when she found it. "So which one of my darling children put this here for me?" she bellowed, showing me the clipping. "I am perfectly able to drive, and I'll drive as long as I choose! I was driving long before any one of them! Do you think I'm gonna sit around and wait for them to take me places?"

Her health was another thing. She'd always been strong and worked hard. She prided herself on how much she could still do at age eighty-three. When the colder weather came she carried all her porch furniture to the basement herself. Everybody told her they would have done it for her, but she seemed sort of secretly pleased that she was able to do it. One day her daughter found her balanced on a chair getting down her stored Christmas tree ornaments. "Mother!" she reprimanded. "Why didn't you wait and let me get those for you? You break your hip and you'll really be sorry!" She seemed to like to prove something by doing things that were somewhat risky.

Now here she was, edging into the topic she kept avoiding with her kids. "I know I need to make some changes. But I can hardly bear the thought. Those kids of mine think I don't know? They have no idea how much energy it takes to keep on going. I never dreamed I'd feel like this. When I was younger and thought about getting older, I swore to myself that I'd be rational about it, that when the time came I'd pack up my stuff and find some smaller place where I wouldn't be a bother. It's a whole different thing when you get there." She picked up a cup in her gnarled old hands, poured some tea and sat down with me.

"I really can't believe I'm this old! I know I've got to get out of this house. I can't keep up with it, and I'm sure not going to pay somebody else to do it for me. But look at this place. How can I leave here? We came here not long after we were married. Every single square inch of this place has been touched by somebody dear to me. It's like this old place is built into me, part of me. It'll be like leaving myself and everybody precious behind. You might as well tear me apart.

"Sometimes I sit here at night all by myself and just look around. The old place comes alive with memories. I can see the kids when they were little and even hear their voices. I remember Christmases here, and see everybody around the tree opening presents, and at the table for dinner. My mom and dad used to visit us here. I didn't look so bad then either! But look at me now. Nobody pays any attention to how an old lady looks. Who cares?

"All these memories and the thought of leaving make me feel like I'm gonna be washed away on all my feelings. Sometimes it feels like my heart will break with love and sadness. It's all so bittersweet. I can't believe how fast it's all gone. And I feel really a hodge-podge of things—like I don't want it all to end, and then again, that it's really okay. I don't want to let go of my independence. I've been the mother, and I've made the decisions, and now they all want to tell me what to do.

"I do have some regrets. Sometimes all the arguments and hard times come back, too. I know I tried to control everything. And usually I did. You know that old saying, 'Mama ain't happy, ain't nobody happy?' Well, that was me lots of times. We had a good marriage, but I think I could have been a little easier to live with. One of these days I'd like to tell the kids how sorry I am that I was too hard on them at times. I hope they forgive me.

"Do you know what the worst thing would be for me? To have to go to a nursing home. I just dread that. I've always dreamed of living out my life in my own home, and that's what I'd like best. But I know some of the things I do are risky, and I'm not taking very good care of myself. I really don't want to fall and break anything. That would get me to a nursing home for sure. I'd rather wind up living with one of my kids—which I always said I'd never do—than go to a nursing home.

"Oh, well. I know I've been rambling on and on to you. It helps to get it all out in the open, though it doesn't solve anything. It's been inside me so long it feels like a big weight on my heart. Maybe one of these days I'll get up enough courage to say it's time to go. But I don't know. If I thought life was gonna get easier as I got older, I sure was mistaken. I cry now more than I think I ever did in my whole life."

In fact, as she spoke, tears formed in her eyes.

IF WE LEARN TO BE AWARE OF FEEL-
INGS WITHOUT GRASPING OR AVER-
SION, THEN THEY CAN MOVE
THROUGH US LIKE CHANGING
WEATHER, AND WE CAN BE FREE TO
FEEL THEM AND MOVE ON LIKE THE
WIND.

Jack Kornfield

5

Remember the Ways You Have Dealt With Earlier Losses

AFTER AWHILE YOU LEARN . . .

THAT YOU REALLY CAN ENDURE

THAT YOU REALLY ARE STRONG

AND YOU REALLY DO HAVE WORTH.

AND YOU LEARN. AND YOU LEARN.

WITH EVERY FAILURE YOU LEARN.

Anonymous

Much of our personal growth and many of the miracles of our lives have come after experiencing loss. Each of us has experienced many losses in life. Wisdom tells us that to live long means to have died many times. We know that the pattern of the universe is one of death to life to death to life over and over again. So all new life and growth comes through some undoing.

One of the things that can be helpful to us when we experience a new loss is to remember the ways we've dealt with losses in the past. What helped us then? If we reminisce about some prior time when we felt done in by a loss, can we also remember what helped us through? Some typical responses that I've heard include:

- "It was the support of my family and friends."
- "For me it was my faith."
- "I don't know any one thing. I'd have to say it was a group of things working together."

Insight and hope may be gained by "sitting at the feet of our own lives and being taught by them." We can learn what we've done well and healthily to help us through past grief, and we can also learn what may have kept us mired in our grief or even slowed down our healing.

We are creatures that live by habits. We begin as tiny children learning how to cope with life. We learn early on to imitate and follow what we see around us in our families. Such imitation can be for good or for ill. Mothers and fathers, older brothers and sisters, and other family members provide patterns for us to follow. These family members don't even realize that little eyes and minds are watching and learning—without even being told. For example, many of us grew up in a time when children were sent off to a friend's home so as not to be around grieving family members. Now, as adults, that experience may have taught us to avoid grief. Often, young boys were taught different lessons about how to grieve than young girls.

Besides imitating others, we also learned what to do when something we did was given affirmative attention, when words of praise or another reward came our way because we behaved a certain way. For example, a mother says, "Billy, you handled your move to a new school just like a man. You were so strong, and I didn't even see you cry!" Afterwards we tend to continue doing things that way throughout our lives, even for losses like death.

Most often we're not completely aware that we have formed such habits. Unless we wake up to them at some time in our lives and think about what and why we do what we do, we will continue using the styles we've learned and were reinforced in our earlier years. These styles can be good or bad.

We can profit by thinking specifically about our own history of losses.

Until we become conscious of how we go about our grieving—the style we've learned and used through our own lives—we will continue to use the same patterns. If they're healthy patterns, we need to take note of them and reinforce them. If they're unhealthy or working against us, we need to recognize that and learn new and healthier ways.

When Sue's husband died, her family and friends were amazed at her ability to handle everything. She greeted all the guests at the funeral home, saw to it that they were introduced to each other, and organized a big family meal after the funeral. For months after the death she was everywhere, involving herself in whatever needed attention. She returned to work quickly and brushed away expressions of condolence. "That's life," she'd say briskly to people who asked her how she was doing. "You can't stop and feel sorry for yourself. There's lots to be done."

Only after a near collapse several months later would Sue talk with a counselor. There she quickly came to see that her family's style for grieving from the time she had been small was to get busy. "Don't sit around feeling sorry for yourself," she remembered her grandmother saying after her grandpa had died. She had been given chores around the house to prepare things for the funeral. None of her family seemed to show any sorrow. She also remembered when she was eight and her all-time favorite dog was hit by a car. Her mother said to her, "Now wipe your eyes and don't feel sad. It's just a dog."

Family styles are important to think about, as are religious styles. Sometimes religious styles and teachings have been directed at avoiding grief by attempting to replace it with thoughts of an afterlife and reward. Some people may have come to see grieving as an indication of lack of faith. One hospital chaplain told of an older woman who was quite stoical as her husband lay dying, showing no signs of sorrow. Hard as he tried to support her in some expression of her grief, the absence of even a tear puzzled him. Then one evening, as her husband's death drew close, she began to softly cry into her handkerchief, almost hiding what she was doing. At that moment her pastor arrived and in a loud voice proclaimed, "Mrs. Jones is a strong believer. She knows God wipes away every tear and keeps us from feeling sorry for ourselves." Obviously he had never read the story of Jesus weeping at the tomb of his friend, Lazarus.

Experiencing loss is part of being human. Expressing emotion and following our religious beliefs can be necessary and healthy parts of grieving. While our faith may tell us about resurrection and new life, our humanness tells us we need to grieve in order to make our way through loss. A sign of wisdom is our willingness to never stop learning from our grief.

LIFE IS NOT THE WAY IT'S SUPPOSED TO BE. IT'S THE WAY IT IS. THE WAY YOU COPE WITH IT IS WHAT MAKES THE DIFFERENCE.

Virginia Satir

Remember the Ways You Have Dealt With Earlier Losses

- Reminisce about times in your childhood when loss or death came into your family. What do you remember about how your mother and father grieved? Did the family talk about the loss? Was it okay to express your emotion?

- What were you taught about religious meaning in times of loss and death? What do you still believe? Does your religious belief help you and give you comfort? Or are there other reactions that your religious beliefs bring up for you?

- If a person's death is still difficult for you, select a photo or memento that reminds you of the one lost. Let it help you touch what remains difficult. Try to create a new way to grieve that loss now.

- How do you typically grieve? Can you see any connection in the ways you grieve to the ways you were taught, or the ways your family grieved?

- What helps you make your way through grief when loss comes into your life?

- What ways do you think you could do better with your grieving?

LOSS PROVIDES AN OPPORTUNITY TO TAKE INVENTORY OF OUR LIVES, TO RECONSIDER PRIORITIES, AND TO DETERMINE NEW DIRECTIONS.

Gerald Sittser

It Would Have Been Okay

When she was a little girl, Ruth was sent off to live with an aunt. She was a sickly child who needed special attention, and her family was poor. When her dad came to visit, a rare event, she was excited and remembers reaching out to him from her bed when he came through the door. But her arms remained empty, as did his, since he never responded to her aching to be hugged.

Now in her eighties, she recalls, "That's the way my whole family was. Nobody ever showed much emotion. If you did get excited about something, or were sad, or angry, nobody paid much attention. It seemed to have no effect on anybody else. In fact, it was sort of pointless to show anything. Sometimes, I remember, it would do the opposite of what you wanted it to do. I remember once taking my mother's hand when we were walking down the street. It felt good to hold on to her, warm and close. She shook me off and said, 'What's the matter? Can't you walk by yourself?' That felt worse than if I hadn't reached out to her in the first place."

Here she was now, with a sort of dreamy look as her eyes wandered out the window to nowhere in particular. Her daughter was visiting, offering a loving sounding board for reminiscing about her life, rambling around through its ups and downs. "I think it was pretty early when I must have decided there was no point to showing my feelings. As I look back, it's almost like I threw the switch into the off position. I worry sometimes that I wasn't affectionate enough with you kids. But it never entered my mind then. I just did the job and kept my feelings out of it. It was too painful to put them out there and get them slapped down.

"One time I broke my rule. Only one time. It was when your father left me for another woman. First I couldn't believe it, and then I was devastated and cried my eyes out. I pleaded with him to stay, but got the same old response that I always did. None. I think it was cemented in then.

"Later, when I found another man who was interested in me, I guess I still had a strand of my old hope, so I made one more try at it. I summoned up all my courage and called your father. I asked if there was any chance that we might be able to get back together. He said no. He 'didn't want the responsibility.' Those were his words. I'm not sure just what that meant. But I knew he didn't want me.

"So I married that other guy, and it was disastrous. And you know I married a couple other ones, too. Only one of those marriages was any good. You remember Harry. Harry really loved me. Treated me like I was somebody. I'm not sure I ever really showed him how important he was to me. I see now it was too risky for me, but I think I really did love him. If I'd had a longer time with him maybe I could have opened up a little bit more. But he went and died on me after only five years. So it sort of proved my theory: don't show anybody what you feel. Or, better yet, don't even feel it."

She grew quiet and rested her head back in the chair. "But Mother," her daughter ventured, "I remember you after Harry's funeral. You really shocked me. We came back to your house from the church, and you went into his room and started packing up all his clothes and things. I didn't see you shed a tear. You put everything in boxes and told us to get rid of them. It was like you cleaned him out of your life. Just that fast. I didn't understand that."

She stirred only slightly in her chair, perhaps a bit uncomfortable at the memory. "It's beginning to be clear to me only now." Her words came slowly, "Breaking down and crying wouldn't get me anywhere. He was gone. So I just needed to get on with it myself and see what was next. What was the point of even feeling sad? Though I did miss him. I think if I hadn't gotten busy I would have embarrassed myself in front of you kids with my crying." She became quiet.

"It would have been okay, Mother," her daughter said, reaching out. They sat for a few moments in silence, holding onto each other's hand. Then force of habit, years of habit, drew the mother's hand away from the daughter and back into her own lap.

"You know when it hit me?" she turned to her daughter. "Two weeks ago, after I'd been in that car wreck, I was really scared. I could have been hurt bad. It's a wonder I wasn't killed.

"Well, when I went to the Senior Center that week, I told them about my accident. I wanted to get it out of my system. Well, they were all listening, and it felt so good to get it out. And then one of them, Mary, reached out and put her arm around me. I was stunned. But it felt so good at first."

For a few moments the room was quiet as Ruth struggled with her thoughts. Finally, she added, "Then I reached up, and I took her arm away and everybody turned from me, and reached out to Mary." And with a blink of her eye, a tear coursed slowly down Ruth's wrinkled cheek.

WE HAVE TO FIND WAYS TO UNLEARN THOSE THINGS THAT SCREEN US FROM THE PERCEPTION OF PROFOUND TRUTH.

Thomas Moore

Making Peace

K athleen came with a lot of determination and had a specific wish. I could tell she had been thinking about this for a long time. "My mother is old, and even though she's still pretty healthy, I know she probably won't live a whole lot longer. I have been angry with her forever, and I don't know why. We get along okay on the surface, but it's something between us that won't go away. And what I do know is that I'd like to make peace with her before she dies. I don't want to keep on carrying these bad feelings."

We had been talking in a group about how each of us has a history of losses, and how important it is to grieve them and move on. Kathleen said that she felt an underlying anger with her mother for as long as she could remember. "And I think it affects lots of things in my life. It's become almost a life style or a habit for me, and I don't want to do it anymore! Could it be that it's just one of those 'hate your mother' kinds of things?" she asked me before answering her own question. "No, it's something definite that I've been holding onto."

So we set out a plan for the couple days we would be there in the group together, and she began figuring out what the anger was all about. She talked about it and prayed about it. She searched her memory and even dreamed about it. Nothing seemed to come through that helped her to understand her experience.

Then, on the last day, a knock came on my door. There stood Kathleen with tears in her eyes and sadness written all over her face.

"I remember," she said simply.

I welcomed her in.

"I'm the oldest in our family," she began. "What came flooding back to me were memories of being the apple of Mom and Dad's eye. Remembering those times was like a big hug that makes you feel good all over. We did so many things together. Mom and I especially did lots of snuggling, reading stories, and playing. I remember feeling so loved and having so much warmth and affection.

"Then something happened when my sister was born. I was around five. My mom told me, 'You're going to have to take care of yourself now. You're a big girl, and now I have your baby sister to take care of. I can't be spending as much time with you.'

"That was it. That was the turning point. I honestly don't ever remember her holding me again. It was like being thrown out of paradise, having to fend for myself. That experience colored my whole life. I've been angry in some way for as long as I can remember, so I knew whatever it was came really early in my life. But I must have blocked the whole thing out of my awareness. It just made me so angry.

"You know, I think she was so matter-of-fact about taking my sister into what I thought was my place, that I probably never did grieve over all that. And I think that's why I've been pretty unfinished with all kinds of things that have gone on in my life. And I seem to get angry about so many things.

"I don't think Mom even had a clue about how hard that was on me. I still don't think she has. I'm sure she's felt my anger over all these years, but she's never even asked me why I'm always so angry with her.

"So I guess what I did was turn my normal anger into a lifestyle, and I've lived with that anger, and off of that anger for years. Now I'm not sure what to do about it. I wonder if I can bring it to her and talk about it with her. But I bet she'll be the same as she's always been—pretty unaware. She'll say, 'Angry? Why, honey, what have you got to be angry about? You've always been my number one girl.'

"But at least I know now, and I can stop my part in all this. I do love her, and I do want to be at peace with her. After all these years."

HEALING . . . DOES NOT COME FROM INCREASING THE AMOUNT OF LIGHT IN OUR LIVES, BUT FROM REACHING INTO THE SHADOW AND DRAWING UNRECONCILED ELE-MENTS OF OURSELVES INTO THE LIGHT WHERE THEY CAN BE HEALED.

Greg Johanson and Ron Kurtz

6

Ask Your God to Help You in Your Grieving

MY GOD, MY GOD, WHY HAVE YOU

FORSAKEN ME?

Psalm 22

Through all the years I've been dealing with dying persons or those in the midst of loss and grief, all but a few have brought God into the struggle. Many have found their relationship with God to be their strongest support or consolation in the time of grief. Even with those who said they were opposed to religion, God seemed to make an appearance in our discussions, even though the mention of God was at times somewhat negative. I would face questions like: "If God cares about people, why is this happening?" or "Why would God allow this suffering?"

In the midst of difficult times, our urge to find meaning for life and to wonder about the meaning of suffering seems strongest. Because we are able to "fix" so many problems in life, we feel helpless when we cannot undo our suffering. We always try to understand why: Why did this happen? Why did this happen to me? Am I being punished for something?

And when we have engaged in such searches, we've tended to locate God somewhere in the middle of the experience as a way of trying to make sense of the loss. We realize that a power exists outside of us, that we are inserted into a universe that is bigger than we are, and that this power gives us things and takes them away.

All religions attempt to provide answers to questions of suffering and death. Sometimes, however, there is no answer to loss and death other than that "they are part of life." Homicide, suicide, other tragic and catastrophic losses may challenge our searching and may never be resolved satisfactorily. Bad things do happen to good people, and we may never fully understand why. So both searching for meaning and giving up the need to understand play roles in healthy grieving. Trying to make sense of loss and death can even bring us to some peace.

In a bereavement group, Marta said, "I need to believe God took my husband away. That's the only way it can be okay for me. If I thought God didn't have anything to do with it, I couldn't handle it." And in the same group, Elise immediately came back with, "Oh, not me! I don't for a minute think God comes and takes people away. I think that's just the way it is in life. You live and you die. And I think God is walking right here with us and helping us when times are hard and we have to let go of somebody." A third woman, Catherine, added, "All I know is that God loves us, and I turn to God for help in all my troubles."

All three of these women are good examples of how uniquely we each come to believe or to not believe in God (or any other name we use for a Higher Power), and how what we believe plays a role when we try to make sense of suffering. Through so many experiences of our lives—what we were taught, how we were treated, how our parents and other important people in our lives dealt with us—we come to develop our unique image of God.

I once heard a religious teacher say that there are as many "gods" as there are people in this world. I think what the teacher meant was that each of us develops our own image of who God is. Though each of the above women had a different image of God's role in her life, each one claimed to have found help through her own belief.

Some beliefs in the area of religion and God, however, could have just the opposite effect from healing. If, for example, a person's image of God were of a vengeful power out to punish and destroy, little consolation or help would probably be found in a time of suffering.

Rather, we might reflect on some ways that God and religion can help us in our time of grief. For example, the scripture or sacred writings of all the great world religions address suffering and death. These sacred books hold stories, prayers, and thoughts that offer wisdom in difficult times.

The sacred writings remind us that sickness and suffering, aging and death are part of the human condition, part of the natural order of things. Sickness and death come to the just and the unjust, the kind and the mean. We don't get off for good behavior. Life is simply built this way.

In these sacred writings we often find some passages with which we identify more than others do. Some passages speak the words that could be our own. In the Hebrew scriptures we find the book of Psalms crying out with words like, "My God, my God, why have you deserted me? . . . I call all day, my God, but you never answer." Marilyn, mother of a son who had died in an attempted robbery in the store where he worked, said, "These are exactly my words. I feel like God is gone, that I've been totally deserted. And yet I keep praying them."

The book of Isaiah consoles with the words, "The Lord God will wipe away the tears from all faces." Jenny said, "Sometimes when things have been really hard, I like to just sit and think about those words, about how my hope is that someday we won't ever have to cry anymore."

Sometimes we find help and direction in our difficulties by looking to religious figures who can point the way for us in our loss and grief. Siddhartha Gautama, the Buddha, shows us the way of simply being with our suffering. While it certainly can be helpful to search for cures and solutions, often the time comes when we must learn to simply live with what is. The Buddha teaches us to do that.

The Jewish prophets suffered great rejection by their own people. Their words and their lives can be excellent models for us in our suffering. The book of Job struggles with questions of the goodness and justice of God in the face of what seems to be undeserved suffering and intense and meaningless loss. In the Christian tradition, as he wept at the tomb of his friend Lazarus, Jesus not only shows us how to grieve, but he also teaches and shows us how to die. His own suffering and death is the central mystery of the Christian faith.

People who have experienced loss and grief will often say that their belief in God was the single most significant source of help. Over and over I have heard grieving people make comments like,

- "I never could have made it without God's help."

- "It was mostly my faith that got me through it."

- "God was with me every step of the way."

It is wise, then, like many others around us and those who have gone before us, to look to the wisdom of the ages, to the God of the Universe, to find support, consolation, and help in our grief.

GOD OF ALL CONSOLATION, GRANT

TO THOSE WHO SORROW THE SPIRIT

OF FAITH AND COURAGE, THAT THEY
MAY HAVE THE STRENGTH TO MEET
THE DAYS TO COME WITH STEAD-
FASTNESS AND PATIENCE; NOT SOR-
ROWING WITHOUT HOPE, BUT
TRUSTING IN YOUR GOODNESS.

A New Zealand Prayerbook

Ask Your God to Help You in Your Grieving

- Praying words from your wisdom tradition can console you in your grieving. Ponder these each day. One way of bringing these words of consolation into your daily life is to select a short phrase and spend a few moments reciting the words silently in harmony with your breathing—for example, "Be not afraid, I am with you always." As you breathe in say, "Be not afraid," and as you breathe out say, "I am with you always."

- What is your image of God? Is your God punishing, loving, close, distant, judging, or welcoming? What words would you use to describe God? If you belong to a particular religious tradition, review the sacred literature of your tradition. Chances are that you will find images of God that may help you in your grieving.

- Imagine yourself sitting before a God who loves you and wants to "wipe every tear from your face." Pour out to God all your pain and sadness. If you are feeling angry and despairing about your loss, choose words that express those feelings and imagine yourself being able to say them to a God who still loves you no matter what you say.

- Is there a significant religious figure who is a model for you or whom you would like to take as a model? What is it about this person that speaks to you and offers wisdom and consolation in your grieving?

- Choose a few words from some spiritual or religious writing that speaks to you and spend some time simply letting those words rest in your mind. Here is one ancient method of meditating on sacred texts:

  - Relax in silence for some time, breathing deeply and slowly.

  - Slowly read the passage; let your heart work through it, tasting words or phrases that seem to invite special attention.

  - Repeat over and over again one line that seems to be especially important for you; let its import become clear to you.

  - Read the passage again—slowly, attentively.

  - In your mind and heart, formulate a one-word or short-phrase response to the reading. Recite the word or phrase response to the reading in harmony with your breathing.

  - Slowly read the passage once again.

  - Ponder the reading with this question in mind: How does this reading touch my life at this particular time?

  - End with a quiet period, a prayer, or just thoughts of thankfulness.

I DID NOT BECOME A RABBI BECAUSE I BELIEVE. I BECAME A RABBI BECAUSE I COMMITTED MY LIFE TO NEVER GIVING UP SEARCHING AND YEARNING FOR GOD. I AM A RABBI BECAUSE

THERE IS IN ME, AS THERE IS IN YOU,
A CHILD, A CHILD THAT KNOWS THAT
SOMEWHERE WE ARE NOT ALONE,
THAT THIS WORLD IS BATHED IN MIR-
ACLES, AND THAT FOR EVERY PAIN
THERE IS BEAUTY, FOR EVERY LOSS
THERE IS LOVE, AND FOR EVERY
WASTE THERE IS WONDER.

Rabbi David Wolpe

New Life

Sandra still remembers what she was doing on the day the doctor's office called and said her routine mammogram showed a growth. Everything became sort of blurred after that though, except for the pain of the needle biopsy. The rest was all jumbled together: first the diagnosis that surprised even the doctor at its "aggressiveness," then the flurry of discussions and decisions about the experimental treatment, doing the procedures to be sure her heart could handle it, and then beginning the awful chemotherapy.

"For a while I was just numb," Sandra recalled. "I was forty-two years old, had kids in high school, a marriage that had been in jeopardy for a couple years, and had already been questioning what I was going to do with myself and my life. Then this. Cancer. And not just a simple cancer, not something ordinary or routine, as if cancer can ever be considered routine. But this awful, devastating kind that was like an internal beast set out to devour me from the inside.

"I'd already been feeling like there was a beast on the outside of me, devouring the life I thought I had. My husband was doing me in—not to mention himself. He was drinking a lot, didn't come home some nights, and when he was there all we did was fight. Everything was falling apart. I was seriously looking at divorce, though wanting to get the kids out of school first.

"When this hit, once I got through the initial, bad dream part of it, a strange sort of something came over me. It was almost like the experience was bringing my life into some kind of focus, and I began to see that my life really didn't have focus at all. Nothing seemed to be a place of strength for me. I had nothing to hold me up. I sort of lived from day to day going along without anything solid."

Sandra's eyes glanced out the window and rested on the red and gold fall leaves dancing in the soft breeze. She seemed for a moment to be in another place. Seeing her curled up in a comfy chair, her legs tucked under her, she looked ten years younger than her now fifty-one years. Her face was shining and healthy and there was no hint of the cancer that nearly took her life. It turned out that the same cancer that nearly killed her was also the instrument for giving her back her life, even more life than she had experienced before.

"Things changed," she continued. "My cancer went into remission with the treatment, but I kept searching for a cure of another kind. I knew something was missing, and I became bound and determined to find it.

"When the doctor said, 'live one day at a time,' it hit me that I wasn't really living on any day. I'd been rushing around, as busy as everybody else, involved in all kinds of things, and really feeling sorry for myself because of the mess at home, but I think now I was really lost. And if my time was coming to an end, I didn't want to be lost.

"So, as soon as I went into remission, I went back to school. I thought if I learned more, that might be it. I'd feel like I'd accomplished something. I did go through with the divorce I'd been moving toward. My kids were doing fine now. One had graduated and was in college, and the other was a senior. I knew I had done well with them, but it kept coming back to me. Who was I? Where was I going?

"Then, like a bolt from the blue, the cancer came back. Talk about the rug being pulled out from under you. The high I'd been riding, thinking I was getting somewhere, evaporated, and I was back in the depths again, fearing for my life.

"This time though, something was different. I realized that my questions and my searching hadn't been useless. I think the searching itself was helping me. When I was in the waiting room on a visit to see the doctor a woman was sitting next to me and we started talking. She had breast cancer, too, but I've never met anyone so peaceful. She wasn't much older than I was, but I felt more calm just sitting by her.

"She gave me a huge gift that pushed me in the direction I think I was already going. She said to me, 'I don't think I could have handled this without God at my side.' And I didn't know what to say. Our mother saw to it that we went to Sunday school when we were kids, but church never became anything important to me. But this woman wasn't just talking about going to church. She was telling me about a God who was alive for her, a God who was 'at her side.'

"That's when I started thinking, 'Maybe that's why I'm feeling so peaceful while I'm sitting here next to her!' Maybe God was by my side, too, sitting right there in the waiting room. And by my side when I was feeling rotten, too. And maybe my wanting my life to make sense was leading me in the direction of getting closer to God."

I could see the excitement growing in Sandra as she kept talking about her search. Her feet were now on the floor, and she was leaning forward in her chair, looking right at me. It was obvious she really wanted me to understand.

"It's really beyond 'going to church' for me," she continued. "In fact that's only one part of it. I did find a church that seems to fill what I need now, and I go pretty regularly. But I've found that lots of spiritual help comes from other places, too. I've belonged to an Al Anon group for years, and it now has become more meaningful than ever. I go there as much as I go to church! And I read a lot—good things—and pray, too, every day. I'm more at peace than I've ever been in my life.

"It was funny with my cancer coming back. The doctor told me they could give me more chemo, but that it was harsher than the first stuff, and would give me only a fifty percent chance of going into remission again. I asked if I had a chance to live if I didn't take it, and he said that yes I did. So I chose not to do it. I thought I'd take my chances, and you know, I'm doing fine again. Who knows how long I'll be this way, but it's been almost ten years since we first found cancer.

"The important thing is that life is different now. I don't feel like I'm at loose ends anymore. I'd still like to stay healthy and live a long time yet. I'm a grandma now, but I'm also closer to God than I think I've ever been, and that's wonderful. I know that now, and it helps me through the times when things get tough."

YEARNING FOR GOD IS THE HUNGER THAT MOST OFTEN GOES UNRECOGNIZED IN OUR LIVES. OTHER HUNGERS ARE SATISFIED, SOMETIMES ON AN EPIC SCALE. BUT THEY ARE NOT ENOUGH.

Rabbi David Wolpe

God Talk

"I wasn't indifferent to God. I hated him. As you all know I was raised in what everybody thought was such a religious family, and on the outside that's what we acted like. We always went to church, and sat in front of everybody. Mom and Dad and all of us kids lined up in a row—all dressed up. We prayed before meals and at bedtime. Oh, yeah, we looked like the typical American family. Little did anybody know what went on at home. And if anybody did know, they sure didn't do anything about it. If only they had! How different life would have been."

Sarah was part of a group of women who had been abused and who had been working for years to undo some of the harm that had been done. When the group first came together more than ten years before, it took a lot to even get them to open up, but after all this time together and a growing trust and care for each other, more and more of their stories were coming out. Tonight they'd decided to talk about God in their lives.

All six of the women had suffered abuse as little children—several before they were out of their cribs. They talked about how skewed their lives had been, and, in the midst of everything else, how much they all had felt abandoned by God. "It was like I was either invisible or didn't matter," Jan spoke up. "Not only to God, but to everybody. Not even my mother did anything to help me."

Many of them, once they'd grown up, had nothing more to do with God or religion. The general consensus was that if there really was a God, how could such a supreme power let such awful things happen to them. The group would not even talk about a *loving* God. They associated God to be more like their fathers who didn't care what they felt or what happened to them. God was on their abuser's side. Not theirs. There was no love.

Every time the group got onto this subject there were tears, and often great anger. Today Sarah wanted to say something more. "I'm moving into new territory with God." She paused a moment and continued, "At least I think it's about God. Maybe I don't want to call where I'm going by that name though. I think I just want to talk about being spiritual. The more work I've done, and the more I read and think, the more I know I'm a spiritual person, like all of us are. I guess God is part of that.

"I'm still fighting with this, but it's getting to me. I don't know how to explain it, but I think I really hated God because I so much wanted to be loved. I thought God could help me and I wasn't helped. That's why I think I wasn't indifferent. God was too important even while I hated him. I began wondering why that was so. It struck me that there must be more to God than just what I was taught.

"I heard somebody on the TV news say, 'God was with me. I was saved from death in that crash.' And I started thinking: Does that mean God wasn't with the people who died? And I don't think that's true. But if that's not true, then maybe God wasn't just forgetting about me when I was being hurt. Maybe God doesn't act the way we think sometimes.

"The whole thing is sort of confusing, but it makes me think that maybe I've got a lot more to learn about God, and where God is when things are tough. Maybe God's been there all along, walking with me through the muck."

Barbara was puzzled by Sarah's words and said, "Hey, Sarah, you're confusing me. You're way beyond me. I've still been wondering why God let my life be like that. And you're saying maybe God didn't let it, it just was?" Barbara asked, with a puzzled look on her face. "Why are you letting God off the hook like that?"

"I don't think there is a hook, Barbara," Sarah began. "I just think that maybe my healing is somehow connected with God, or maybe I should say it another way. Maybe by opening up to God, who I'm pretty sure is all around, maybe I'll find some help to make it through all this. Maybe I'm the one who has to change, not God. Maybe God's waiting for me with all kinds of healing, if I just open myself up to receive it."

THOUGH THE MOUNTAINS LEAVE THEIR PLACE AND THE HILLS BE SHAKEN, MY LOVE SHALL NEVER LEAVE YOU NOR MY COVENANT OF PEACE BE SHAKEN SAYS THE HOLY ONE, WHO HAS MERCY ON YOU.

The Prophet Isaiah

7

Learn the Lessons
of Everyday Losses

AT FIRST WE THINK WE CAN OUT-
RUN THE DEATH ASPECT OF THE
LIFE-DEATH-LIFE NATURE. THE
FACT IS WE CANNOT. IT FOLLOWS
RIGHT ALONG BEHIND US, BUMPETY-
BUMP, THUMPETY-THUMP, RIGHT
INTO OUR HOUSES, RIGHT INTO
OUR CONSCIOUSNESS. IF IN NO
OTHER WAY, WE LEARN OF THIS
DARKER NATURE WHEN WE CON-
CEDE THAT THE WORLD IS NOT A
FAIR PLACE . . . . YET IF WE LIVE AS
WE BREATHE, TAKE IN AND LET GO,
WE CANNOT GO WRONG.

Clarissa Pinkola Estes

No matter how much we would love to avoid loss in
life, we cannot. The universe flows in a pattern of
life-death-life. The world—both around us and within

us—is subject to the laws of nature. Everything is in constant process: a constant cycle of birth, growing, developing, coming to fullness, diminishing, and then dying. This all repeats itself over and over.

When pressed, we acknowledge the life-death-life cycle, but we never seem to learn how to really live with it. We love the upswings of its natural movement. We take great delight in the birth and raising of our children and when we ourselves also grow, develop, learn, and prosper. Our attempts to cope with the downswings prove more difficult. Most of us would prefer only one half of this cycle.

In essence, what we hold is, "I'll take the side of new life and growth, but I don't want the other side, the side of diminishment and loss." This is impossible. Life and death come together as two sides of the same reality.

When we don't allow ourselves even to be aware that reality holds both life and death, growth and loss, we add another burden to our suffering. We naturally look to place blame for our losses. Our tendency is to see the downswing of the cycle as only coming into our lives when we've done something wrong, are being punished, have somehow fallen into bad luck, or are being treated badly by another. An elderly woman afflicted with cancer commented to me one day, "I think I've been a wolf in sheep's clothing." When I asked her what that meant, she said, "I always believed you get out of life what you put into it, and I thought I was living a pretty good life. But I guess I wasn't, or this wouldn't have happened to me."

In our struggles for meaning, we frequently look for reasons. We tend to ask both questions, "Why is this happening?" and its related, "Why is this happening to me?" The heavens seem to clearly shout back, "Why not?"

When we develop an understanding of the life-death-life cycle we come to see that none of us is immune from loss and the suffering that accompanies it. All we have to do is look around us and we see that loss is one half of the process of life. New life can only come when there is a letting go of what was there before. This is the story of human existence from beginning to end.

Notice the seasons of the year as they cycle through the new birth of spring, the fullness of summer, the bittersweet diminishing of fall, and the death of winter. Notice the moon that never stops in its progression from new moon to first quarter to fullness to third quarter to new moon again. This is the same way we live through in our own lives. Everything keeps moving.

New life only comes through letting go of the old; in every sphere of our being this pattern plays out. Baby teeth must give way to adult teeth. Ideas can't grow unless we're willing to let go of prior ideas. Education and learning replace ignorance. Throughout our lives we pass through a number of psychological growth periods, each with its own tasks, each asking us to let go of what was before. We must regularly move through transitions or deaths and losses in order to move into the next stage of development. Bereavement is indispensable for growth; a hard truth, but truth nonetheless.

At any time in our lives we are experiencing loss and growth in a variety of guises. In our religious and spiritual lives, we struggle with issues of death and loss. Any kind of spiritual growth always requires the process of leaving and arriving. We may find ourselves arriving at new ideas or increased prowess, and at the same time we may be grieving over loss of a friendship, job, or financial security. In many aspects of our life, we can be at varying points on the life to death to life cycle.

Every day we live with the reality of loss. Unless we die young, all of us will experience thousands upon thousands of losses in life. We already have a whole history of losses that have contributed to forming us into who we are at this moment. It's the way we deal with the losses in our lives that sets us up for who and how we are becoming.

When asked what were the three most important steps toward growth on the spiritual journey, a wise teacher of spirituality once responded, "Awareness. Awareness. Awareness." Perhaps the loss of someone or something important can wake us up to the reality of life and give us a sense of our solidarity with every other human being. We can also learn to live our losses in ways that lead to new life.

SOONER OR LATER EVERY ONE OF

US BECOMES AN EXPERT ON LOSS.

Rabbi David Wolpe

Learn the Lessons of Everyday Losses

• Take some time to observe the natural world around where you live. Notice the pattern of life and death that is evident in the trees and other vegetation. Reflect on the changes in the physical setting that have taken place since you moved there.

• Write your own history of loss. Divide your life into ten-year segments and begin listing the wide variety of losses in your life. Notice how some losses are part of a cluster of losses that occurred at the same time. Keep the list and add to it as you remember more losses.

• Think about how the losses of your life have created you to be who you are now. Remember that it's not the loss itself, but the way you choose to cope with it that contributes to your development.

• What losses in your life have been the most significant? What made them so? Which of these losses were clear steppingstones to new life and growth for you? How so?

THE ONLY TRUST REQUIRED IS TO KNOW THAT WHEN THERE IS ONE ENDING THERE WILL BE ANOTHER BEGINNING.

Clarissa Pinkola Estes

Devastation

I awoke in the middle of an April night to booming thunder and lightning that made my room bright as day. Wondering how much longer this would continue, I turned on the television to find that the worst of the storms were still to come. I tried to go back to sleep, knowing that bad storms always come through this time of year. Nothing to worry about.

Then the severe weather sirens sounded. I convinced my mother that it was best that we take shelter in the basement, just as a precaution. Although we felt kind of silly, I grabbed a flashlight and a hand-held television on the way. As we huddled in the basement waiting for the worst to pass, our nine-year-old Golden Retriever started whining and pacing back and forth. He became almost frantic, and we just couldn't understand why he would not settle down. Until we heard it.

Just like all the stories we heard, it sounded like a freight train pounding down on us. We heard glass breaking and waited for the roof to cave in. This was certainly not just another thunderstorm passing by. A tornado had surprised our neighborhood!

After waiting for the "all-clear" from the weather-man, we slowly climbed the stairs to see that our house was in fact still standing. Just before dawn, we emerged from our house into our front yard to find a disaster. I had only seen such a debacle on the news or in movies. Much of our roof, siding, and shutters were strewn about the lawn. The smaller trees on the sides of our house had been ripped from the ground and tossed a few hundred feet. The giants that had towered at least a hundred feet over our backyard were either broken off or uprooted, leaving holes in the ground fifteen feet deep. Our next-door neighbors had lost the top floor of their home. Personal belongings and garbage were strewn about everywhere.

Were our neighbors injured? My uncle lived a few blocks away from us. Was he hurt? Or worse yet, had anyone died? The questions started simply, but as time went on became more complex. Why did this happen? Why did it have to be my neighborhood? This is just not fair. Why me? Why not someone else? How can I handle this with all the other things that I have to deal with everyday?

But then I began to think. Why not me? Why should this happen to someone else instead of me? Why am I exempt from the destruction that this world can bring? I have no special privilege to skip the trials and tribulations of this world. Even though we did not lose our home, we lost many other things that would change my life forever. Our beautiful trees that once shaded my swing set in the backyard were gone. My home of twenty-three years was significantly damaged. From then on our dog never left my mother's side. He followed her from room to room when she was home and fretted when we were not.

Because of the dreadful storm, I could no longer

enjoy sleeping to the sound of the rain tip-tapping on the roof. The sense of security once provided to me by my home was gone forever.

Ironically, the realization of all we had lost transformed itself into a greater appreciation for all the things we did have. I still had my wonderful family and friends who spent many days helping us with the endless task of putting our lives back together. My community truly banded together after the tornado. Police and other city workers came from all over Cincinnati to pitch in and assist with the clean up. Local churches provided extra workers to help cut wood or shovel dirt. I found that I enjoyed planting trees and watching them grow. Instead of occasionally waving hello, we are now on a first-name basis with our neighbors. We all share so much more in common now— most importantly, life.

Looking back on all that has happened, I know that I have changed. I know that I am vulnerable. I know that my life can be turned upside down in an instant. The naive, sheltered person that I once was no longer exists.

But I also know that I am strong. I am a survivor. The next time I am faced with something that seems like it is too much for me to handle, I will know that it is not. I am confident. I know that even when life deals me a lousy hand of cards, I can still make the best of it. Or, as my boyfriend says, when life gives you lemons, make lemonade. Those sayings never made much sense to me until now. I've found that the lemons can be very sweet when put in proper context.

Jennifer Guntzelman

IT IS THE SWAMPLANDS OF THE
SOUL, THE SAVANNAS OF SUFFERING,

THAT PROVIDE THE CONTEXT FOR
THE STIMULATION AND THE ATTAIN-
MENT OF MEANING. AS FAR BACK AS
2500 YEARS AGO AESCHYLUS
OBSERVED THAT THE GODS HAVE
ORDAINED A SOLEMN DECREE, THAT
THROUGH SUFFERING WE COME TO
WISDOM.

James Hollis

Living Losses

The first time my newborn son was placed in my arms we bonded.

He was exactly a month overdue and more physically mature than most infants. His inexperienced eyes met mine, and our souls mingled. Although overjoyed by his birth, the long-term responsibility of having a child was daunting to me. With youthful ignorance on my side, the challenge was accepted. There was so little understanding of what joy and sorrow children bring into a willing heart. It was my fervent wish that this little boy would be loved, cherished, and guided into a responsible adulthood. It was important that, when the time came, he had the tools and the freedom to embrace his own life. Little did I know the many times during this process that grief would knock on my door to help my journey along.

When our son was three, my marriage of six years met the fate of so many, a divorce. Essentially my son was raised by me and surrounded by other women, his aunts and grandmothers. One of my greatest challenges was when my son's father remarried. He and his wife would have him for a variety of outings. It took incredible self-restraint on my part not to muddy their relationship. The grief involved was intense and gripping. Over time, we managed to develop a working friendship. It was difficult to attain, but worth it for my son's sake.

There was the more common grief involving things like the first day of school, a driver's license, girlfriends—all the things that put fear in a mother's heart and gray hairs on her head.

What came as a total shock was when my son announced he was joining the Navy to become a SEAL. The thought shattered the picture I had of my child. He adored animals and was compassionate. He had even written a short story about hunting from a deer's perspective. Now he wanted to become one of an elite Special Forces group that is trained to kill if necessary. As I learned more about the SEALS, I was more grief-stricken, for my son was walking into a world from which I could not protect him. This was a huge loss for me, but obviously something he needed to tackle. It was important for me to make the final cut to the umbilical cord and let my precious child realize his dreams.

The Navy SEAL Training was ferocious. My son rose to its many challenges and completed the program. He now proudly wears the SEAL Trident. Surprisingly enough, because he wanted it so much, I wanted it for him. His wife and I were his strongest supporters. But grief and fear still plagued me as thoughts of his unknown future enveloped my daily activities.

There are gifts to be found in all life's experiences, even the dark times. My son's decision to become a Navy SEAL gave me abundant growth opportunities. It also showed me that I had heavily nurtured my son's feminine energy. He needed to experience his warrior side. Now before me stands a more completely balanced individual. Like a finely tuned instrument, his masculine/feminine energies are in balance. He is the joy of my life. He is a source of great pride for me. As a parent I weathered the ongoing process of life-death, receiving-letting go, happiness-grief. My strong, handsome, self-reliant son is the fruit of my labors. The two things a good mother gives her children are "wings to fly and roots to come home to." I have succeeded.

Suzette Sexson

YOUR GRIEF IS YOUR OWN, ALL THE DAYS OF YOUR LIFE. LET NO ONE DEPRIVE YOU OF IT, NOT EVEN OUT OF LOVE. PAIN IS INSEPARABLE FROM LOVE; THAT IS A TRUTH WE MUST LIVE WITH. IT IS A PROOF OF OUR TRUE INNER REALITY, A JUDGMENT OF OURSELVES, AS TO HOW AND WITH WHAT COURAGE WE FACE AND ACCEPT THAT TRUTH.

Gerald S. Sloyan

8

Choose to Reintegrate Back Into Life

THE TURNING POINT IN GRIEF IS
MARKED WITH A DECISION EITHER
TO MOVE FORWARD—AND IN
DOING SO RELINQUISH THE PAST AS
IT HAD BEEN LIVED WITH THE
DECEASED—OR TO REMAIN IN
THE STATUS QUO, NOT MAKING
CHANGES.

Catherine Sanders

When our lives are turned upside down by loss and grief, we often want to simply withdraw. Early in our grief, that may be just what we need to do. We have little energy or desire to do anything else. The loss fills our mind and heart, and the rest of life seems to have little attraction for us. After our disbelief lifts, we plunge into intense emotions. What we have lost is not coming back. However, if we give ourselves to the grief and move along, eventually, we will come to a time when a decision presents itself: Can I move back into life?

The question may creep up on us, or it may be suddenly clear. "It was like one day the thought came into my mind that I might start getting through this—that it was time," Mary Ann told her grief group. "At first I pushed it away. It felt like I was being disloyal to my husband. I was afraid I'd forget him if I stopped grieving. But gradually it just felt like I needed to move in that direction—like that was the right thing to do. I don't know how else to explain it."

Most people come to a similar time of decision. Dwelling in the midst of grief, allowing it to do its work in us, presents several possibilities. We can choose to stay as we are and continue to grieve indefinitely, pretending that nothing will change in our lives. We can continue to withdraw and begin a downward spiral away from life. Or we can plow through all the pain and bring ourselves back into living our lives, albeit without the person or job or situation that we've lost.

Even when we don't face loss, we often don't see life as being made of choices. Whenever loss does enter our lives, we do make choices, though often not very consciously.

A psychiatrist once remarked that we often live our lives like we're reading a novel, waiting to see how it all comes out in the end. We miss the fact that we ourselves are the authors! To make our way out of grief, we need to realize that we are the only ones writing the next chapter in our life's story. We have a lot to say about where we go from here. We may not have any control over the reality of the death or loss, but we do have choices about how we deal with it.

Every day we're making such choices that either lead us to growth and new life or diminish us in some way. For example, consider two brothers who chose different lifestyles. Phil, the older of the two, had finished college with a degree in education, taught in a high school, and was working on his master's degree. He and his wife had two young children who were the joy of their lives. He worked hard at his marriage and to be a good father.

Phil's brother Jerry, slightly younger, had a history of drug and alcohol abuse. Jerry had dropped out of college in his freshman year, and showed no interest in returning. Though he'd held several jobs through the course of the years since school, none of them lasted. His bosses said he wasn't dependable and that he seemed uninterested in his work.

One day a friend of the brothers asked Phil what it was that got him to where he was in life. Phil's response came quickly, "Well, my dad was an alcoholic and beat up on us when we were kids. I sure didn't want to live my life like that." Later in the week when this same friend ran into Jerry, he asked how he got where he was in life. Jerry's response also came quickly, "Well, my dad was an alcoholic and used to beat up on us when we were kids. He never gave me a chance to make anything of myself."

Both of the brothers experienced the same loss in their lives. Neither had control over what happened to them as children. How they chose to deal with their circumstances differed sharply. One chose life, and the other death.

After any loss, whether small or enormous, our choice is the same: life or death. No matter what others may say to us, the choice is ours. We can't get off the hook. The words from a classic poster from years ago remain true: "Not to decide is to decide." Whatever we do, even when we try to avoid the responsibility, we are making a decision. If we can consciously opt for life and growth, we enhance our lives.

On the occasion of Viktor Frankl's eightieth birthday, an interviewer asked the eminent Austrian psychiatrist about the most important lessons he had learned in life. Without hesitation, Frankl described a lesson that grew out of his experience in the concentration camps. In the horror of that experience, he became increasingly aware of the various ways in which he and others responded. All of the prisoners were in the same tragic situation, but the responses of the inmates frequently differed widely. Frankl's conclusion was that everything could be taken away from us in life but one thing—our attitude. We are always free, he pointed out, to choose the attitude we have when we face any situation.

So, in loss of any kind, we are presented with a choice of moving toward life and growth or toward death and diminishment. We can decide to choose life.

HE WHO'S NOT BUSY BEING BORN IS

BUSY DYING.

Bob Dylan

Choose to Reintegrate Back Into Life

- Ask yourself: Am I far enough along in my grief to decide where I want to go from here? Am I avoiding making the decision about moving back into life?

- Recognize that every day, every step of the way, you are deciding about something. Recall decisions that you didn't know you were making at the time. List these. Then list choices that you have made recently. Note choices that were life giving and those that may have been life diminishing.

- Consider the fact that there are many ways you could choose to do something, think about something, or feel about something. The *way* you choose tends to become a habit. You can change it.

- Participating in organized activities may help in our reintegration back into life. Consider reaching out to others in need, volunteering in a soup kitchen or food bank, joining a gardening group, or joining with other people in some worthwhile activity.

• Choosing to reintegrate back into life doesn't mean that the struggle is over. Our grieving will continue even as we choose life. Often, choosing life means allowing ourselves to feel all the pain of the loss. Remind yourself that how you deal with the pain is in your hands.

NO ONE IS FREE WHO CANNOT SAY, WITH FEELING, "I AM NOT WHAT HAPPENED TO ME; I AM WHAT I CHOOSE TO BECOME." "I AM NOT MY ROLES; I AM MY JOURNEY." "I AM NOT MY LIMITING EXPERIENCE; I AM THE CREATIVE POWER OF MY POTENTIAL."

James Hollis

Buds

I knew Lisa would be special in my life the first time we met. She came to interview for a job as an occupational therapist at the pediatric clinic where I worked. I am a speech-language therapist. I remember first seeing her standing in the hallway with two friends who had come with her.

Lisa was bubbly and outgoing. She had liquid brown eyes that sparkled in the light. I stopped to welcome her to the clinic and at that moment a deep friendship began.

Both of us were at very different points in our spiritual walks, but it was obvious that we both came together for a reason. From a very rigid boxed-in place, she leaped into her soul journey. Our conversations were filled with wisdom. We shared many insights. It was a beautiful friendship, teeming with love, laughter, and tears. I found it amazing that Lisa really looked to me as a spiritual mentor. At first it was Lisa who followed my lead. But over time it was evident that she was on a spiritual fast track. She sailed on past me spiritually.

Lisa began to embrace the world of nature. This thrilled me because the natural world had always been my closest friend. Now I was blessed with a friend who was open to the lessons creation could offer. Lisa and I went mountain biking, horseback riding, and hiking. Sometimes we would do these things with my son, who had also really taken to Lisa. We always had a great time. This isn't to say that we didn't have our differences, but we always made our way through them.

Lisa totally surprised me when she decided to adopt a dog. She had never had a pet in her life, and wound up with a big, adult male boxer. What a way to start! Boxers are so exuberant and powerful, and this male dog was really strong. Lisa absolutely adored him.

She struggled a long time with what to name her dog. She wanted it to be meaningful. We shared quite an assortment of names before she settled on Chaco, after Chaco Canyon. This was a spiritual place Lisa often went to for answers and she knew "Chaco" had come to her with more lessons to learn.

Five years into this incredible friendship, my dear friend died very unexpectedly. She had gone to lunch with a group of friends from work not long after her thirty-third birthday. They were standing waiting for a table when she told her friends she thought she was going to faint. As they went to help her sit down, Lisa collapsed and died quickly from a blood clot in her leg that broke loose and totally obstructed her pulmonary artery.

Lisa's death was the single, most difficult experience in my life, and I have suffered many profound losses. It put me in touch with my own dark times. It was devastating and overwhelming to me. We had been so connected spiritually, and her death was so unexpected and shocking that for a while I didn't want to go on myself. I couldn't function. I became physically ill.

Spiritually and emotionally I was in very deep grief. I could clearly see that I could have kept giving in to the depression. I really had a choice. Part of my being, my soul, was with Lisa on the other side. But something told me I was on a destructive path. I knew I still had work to do here, that it was clearly not my time. I remember saying to myself that I couldn't just give up and die.

Two events happened before Lisa's death that helped me weather this grievous loss. Three months before her own death, Chaco—by that time fairly old—became very ill and Lisa had a really hard time deciding to euthanize him. We talked and talked and cried and cried. Finally she made the brave choice of setting him free. He was such an important part of her life. She held him, and I held her as the lethal injection was administered.

When Lisa died only months later, it was humbling to think how fortunate it was that he died before she did. Almost like that was part of some greater plan. Most certainly it was.

Eight days before she died, Lisa had gone to Chaco Canyon and had a powerful spiritual experience there. She told me about it only a few days before her death. She said she was sitting there meditating at the canyon when her mother's spirit came to her. Her mother had died seven years earlier, and Lisa missed her greatly.

Lisa said her mother's spirit told her that she would be going home soon, and not to be afraid.

When Lisa told me about it I argued with her, and told her she shouldn't talk like that. She was too young to die. But she said she wasn't afraid and that it would be okay.

I have a picture that Lisa gave me months before her death. She said it reminded her of me. I love it. It's a picture of two brilliant red flowers growing up through a crack in the dry, parched desert earth. The quote on the picture reads, "There are defining moments in a life when faced with the decision to give up or to go on."

For the longest time after Lisa's death I couldn't go mountain biking or do any of the activities we loved to do together. They would bring up too much sorrow. It seemed like profound grief engulfed whatever I was doing.

I can now do those things again, and they bring joy to me rather than sorrow. I make a conscious choice to remember the happy, outrageous memories associated with our friendship. Many times the memories still bring tears. But by deciding to live, my grief process is healthier and more profound.

Although I miss my cherished friend and my life is richer for our relationship, I chose to move forward and I do look to a time when our souls will once again have time to play.

Suzette Sexson

I DO DIMLY PERCEIVE THAT WHILST
EVERYTHING AROUND ME IS EVER
CHANGING, EVER DYING, THERE IS
UNDERLYING ALL THAT CHANGE A

LIVING POWER THAT IS CHANGE-
LESS, THAT HOLDS ALL TOGETHER,
THAT CREATES, DISSOLVES, AND
RECREATES.

Mahatma Gandhi

Born Again

When I spotted him sitting in the rehab department, he was ensconced in the wheelchair that
had almost become part of him. A big grin brightened
his face when he saw me. "Hey, Joan, I got something
to tell you!" he called out. "I'm going to school!" It was
wonderful to see him so upbeat. It hadn't been that way
for quite a while.

When I first met him almost a year before, Michael
was twenty-three years old, a ruggedly good-looking
young adult in the midst of an active, challenging life.
He hadn't settled down as yet. The main goal of his life
was to party, make some money, stay pretty loose, and
not get too committed to much of anything.

His accident brought all of that to a horribly catastrophic end. He had been driving his motorcycle too
fast on the freeway when something—he still didn't
know exactly what—made him lose control.

I had met him in the emergency room. He was crit-
ically injured, with a severed spinal cord.

After the initial shock and emergency treatment,
Mike spent his early days in the hospital in a state of
rage against what had happened. He was alternately
disbelieving, then angry, then weeping like the little
boy who still lived inside him. "I'll show all of you. I
will walk again. I know it. If I work hard, I know I can

do it," he would shout at whoever happened to be with him. He was profoundly and understandably grief-stricken about his damaged body. He felt terribly out of control.

In my job of counseling in the hospital, too often I came into such tragic situations—lives shattered through accidents and serious illnesses. Mike was like so many other young men with similar injuries. The shock of the accident, along with the fact that so often the resulting injuries could not be reversed or repaired, seemed more than most believed they could bear.

Around the time of Mike's injury, another man of about the same age sustained a similar injury, also in an accident on his motorcycle. I found spending time with both of them uncanny. Unaware of each other, here they were in the same setting, grappling with the same injury.

Struggle fills the months and even years after such injuries. Not only does one's broken body need a great amount of attention, but broken spirits need healing, too. Gradually the realization that one will not be able to walk again begins to sink in and the grief intensifies. It is really difficult for a person to make the decision to live again out of a situation like that.

So here was Mike, all excited about telling me he was going back to school. He had enrolled at the university and planned to study business. He was eager to talk about his decision.

"As long as I kept being so mad about what had happened, it was like banging my head against a wall," he said. "It wasn't easy, Joan, but do you know what? I finally decided I had to die to being the guy I used to be. I had to just let go of my old life and be born again in this wheelchair. That was the only way I could move on.

"I still don't like what happened. I wish it didn't happen. But I don't want to stay the way I was—always angry and feeling sorry for myself. I know I can't walk now, but I can do other things. It's still really hard sometimes, but I want to try." Mike was smiling, anticipation shining from his eyes.

It was an especially heartwarming day for me because of news I'd heard not long before visiting Mike. The other young man who was paralyzed had to be rehospitalized after making an attempt to end his life and compounding his injuries.

I HAVE SET BEFORE YOU LIFE AND DEATH. . . . CHOOSE LIFE, THEN, THAT YOU AND YOUR DESCENDENTS MAY LIVE.

Deuteronomy

9

Explore What Binds You to Your Grief

WHEN SORROW COMES, LET US
ACCEPT IT SIMPLY, AS A PART OF LIFE.
LET THE HEART BE OPEN TO PAIN;
LET IT BE STRETCHED BY IT. ALL THE
EVIDENCE WE HAVE SAYS THAT THIS IS
THE BETTER WAY. AN OPEN HEART
NEVER GROWS BITTER. OR IF IT
DOES, IT CANNOT REMAIN SO.

A. Powell Davies

Our grieving can become a way of life. Like a train taking us from one place to another, grieving should be the vehicle that helps us adjust to living without whomever or whatever we have lost. Sometimes, though, we can get caught up in the train ride and have trouble remembering the destination. Similarly we can get caught in grief and have a hard time finding our way out. One danger is turning our grief into a lifestyle that stays with us until we die. It's good to wake up to the choices we make in our grieving, choices that may in fact prolong our grief.

Some people fear putting an end to their grieving. When asked why, many say that if they stop grieving it will be as if they "forgot" the loved one who died. Or to stop grieving would signal that they don't or didn't love the one who died. The grief then takes on the guise of a tribute to the one loved and lost. If these reasons were true, real love would require one to continue grieving forever. Holding on to grief can become synonymous with holding on to who or what was lost.

Another choice we can make that hampers our grief is the choice not to allow the grief to do its work in us. Some grieving persons feel like their emotions—if let loose—would swallow them up. Others may feel that the emotions have a negative effect on themselves and on others. Sometimes, we receive messages from our family discouraging grief. Lucia confided that she couldn't grieve anymore because some family members had told Lucia that her grieving "wasn't right." Ironically, the more Lucia resisted her journey of grief, the longer it took her to move through the process.

Running from our grief and avoiding the reality or the pain of it are the most common ways of trying to get by without letting grief touch us. We can run externally by keeping on the move, by staying busy with a million things, or by jumping into other relationships. We can run internally by burying our feelings, refusing to think about our loss, or by denying the reality.

Grieving a difficult or hurtful relationship can create special problems. Ambivalence about our relationships to people or to jobs or other situations stirs up a whole host of feelings, just like it did while the other person was still alive or while we still held our old job. We struggle with tangled feelings of sorrow and guilt, relief and remorse. At times we may see grief as the way to "pay the price" for our failings in a lost relationship or other losses that were important. We hold on to grief as a way of making up for our inability or unwillingness to right a troubled relationship while the other person is still with us. We might think, "If I feel bad enough, if I keep grieving, things will work out okay."

Our grief may also be prolonged if we've closed ourselves off to other relationships besides the one we've just lost. Harry and Sarah were inseparable through their fifteen-year marriage. Each was all the other wanted, and they rarely socialized with any of their old friends. When Harry died suddenly of a heart attack, Sarah found very few people to turn to in her grief. Everyone had been kept at such a distance that now she was alone in tremendous pain, with no one to turn to.

A new loss may only heighten our vulnerability to other losses. In the classic movie *Brian's Song*, the football player Brian Piccholo was found to have cancer. In the course of treatment he suffered a setback, and said something like, "Even in football, they let you get back on your feet before they knock you down again." Sometimes life doesn't let us "back on our feet." When losses bombard us we may feel submerged in grief and find that our grief may be prolonged.

The loss of a child in death carries an especially poignant suffering for parents and close family. Twenty years after the stillbirth of her firstborn, Ann still remembers his birthday and grieves his loss. Miscarriages may provoke similar emotional pain. For some parents, these deaths may bring about a lifetime of chronic sorrow.

A countless array of circumstances, particular losses, personal choices, and situations may push us toward holding onto or being tied to our grief. Sometimes we feel like our losses are just too much to adjust to, that life is asking more than we can handle. It's understandable that we would want to avoid such painful experiences. It's also important to see that some losses, as with the death of a child, can by their nature prolong grief. In other situations, we may find that our holding on is slowing down or interfering with a healthy resolution of our grief.

Built into the cycle of life to death to life is the need for us to plow right through the pain of grief. When we prematurely stop our grief, we are in essence trying to stop the flow of life. On the other hand, keeping our grief in a tight grasp and continually going in circles without letting go stops the process of life too. Giving ourselves to the sorrow and the emotion helps us move toward the emergence of new life. It may take a long time, and we may feel like we're sinking in the pain. Nevertheless when we grieve well, we say "yes" to the on-going process that brings a new relationship of peace with the one we have lost.

What helps in cutting the ties that slow our grieving?

- Facing squarely the magnitude of our loss.

- Discarding old messages that tell us not to grieve.

- Building a network of supportive relationships.

- Ceasing to place blame.

- Embracing the gift of tears.

THE FRIGHTENING THING ABOUT LOSS IS WHAT WE DO TO OURSELVES TO AVOID IT. WE KNOW WE CANNOT LIVE WITHOUT LOSING, BUT THIS KNOWLEDGE DOES NOT PREVENT US FROM SEEKING TO PROTECT OURSELVES. SO WE NARROW OUR SOULS. WE DRAW OURSELVES TIGHTER AND TIGHTER. NO LONGER OPEN TO THE WORLD WITH ALL ITS HURTS, WE FEEL SAFE.

Rabbi David Wolpe

Explore What Binds You to Your Grief

- Step back from your situation and examine it as if you were watching it unfold in another person or a movie. Is there any way in which you see yourself holding on to grief, not moving along?

- As you look with some perspective at your situation, do you know of anything about your relationship with the person or thing lost that would be slowing your grief?

- Picture the person that died sitting there with you. Imagine a conversation with that person in which you talk—without rancor—about the problematic parts in your relationship. What would the other say to you about the past? What would that person say about the present and future? What would that person want you to do now? What unfinished business in your relationship needs to be addressed? Speak to the person you've lost as though he or she were sitting with you and wanting things to work out well. Write down any insights you received.

- If you're stuck in your grief in any way, what will allow you to move on? Sit quietly with your sorrow or pain, and simply let it be. Then ask your grief for its wisdom. What is the lesson this period of loss is teaching you?

- Release any unhealthy grief from your consciousness. Name and write the parts of grief what you would like to release. Hold the papers in your hand and ponder what keeps you tied to this part of your loss. When you feel ready, burn each paper individually, and as it burns, say, "I release this worry that

has kept me tied to my grief. I ask that it be transformed in the flame and bring me healing."

WHAT LOSS CRIES FOR IS NOT TO BE

FIXED OR TO BE EXPLAINED, BUT TO

BE SHARED AND, EVENTUALLY, TO

FIND ITS WAY TO MEANING.

Rabbi David Wolpe

Anger Intact

From my office on a much-used hallway I could see
the parade of day shift hospital staff on their way
home after work. Every once in a while someone would
look in or stop in and say a word or two. Most were
eager to finish up and return home.

One nurse who I didn't know passed by a couple of
times, walking back and forth, until she got courage to
knock lightly on the open door and asked if she could
come in. "Do you have a little time I could spend with
you?" she asked, her lips quivering with the question.

"Of course," I told her, and directed her to a comfy
chair.

As I came around from closing the office door, I
pulled out a box of tissues and put it near her as the
tears she'd been holding back began to flow. "I'm
sorry," she said. "I didn't think I'd cry. I don't know
where the tears are coming from. I'm more mad than
anything else. It's really Dr. Argent's fault. I scrubbed
for him in the O.R. today, and he screamed at me over
something stupid and I've been furious ever since. I
need to find a job where there aren't any men."

As she talked of the "stupid" thing the surgeon had complained about, Amy's tears dried up and her comment about a workplace with no men began to shift her focus in another direction. "Who do men think they are? God's gift to the human race? The lords and masters of all who can do and say anything they want?"

Amy's eyes became bright and her voice climbed a few decibels as she continued her tirade about men in general, which quickly became the story of her exhusband in particular. In Amy's eyes he ruined her life. She wouldn't even say his name. Throughout our time together that afternoon, her ex-husband was "he," said with concentrated venom. It was obvious that she was filled to the brim with anger towards this man, and that the anger overflowed into every other situation where men were involved in her life.

"No man is ever going to get near me again," she vowed.

As I asked Amy about her experience, trying to understand this huge anger that seemed to consume her, she gradually told the story of their broken marriage. "At first it was good," she said, and then quickly took that back. "No, it was never good. He was lousy from the beginning. I was too quick to fall for him and be taken in by him. If I'd waited even a little while I would have seen what he was really like. He really had me fooled."

For more than fifteen minutes Amy railed against this man to whom she'd been married for five years. The intensity of her anger was tangible in every anecdote she told of their time together. One after another they flowed from her memory. The stories sounded rehearsed, but that quality seemed to be the outcome of repetition. She had probably told them to herself and to others so many times she didn't even have to think. But each little story was another nail in the wall of anger she was building around herself, another reinforcement to keep that wall secure.

Knowing how common anger is in all kinds of loss, especially when the loss is still fresh in our experience, I assumed Amy's divorce was fairly recent. "I'm so sorry, Amy, for all your pain," I offered. "It sounds like the divorce has been very difficult for you. I'm sure it's helpful for you to talk about it and what your experience was like."

"I'm not sure it helps at all," she shot back. "I've been talking about it for nine years now and nothing changes. He still is the lousiest person I've ever met. Nothing can change that."

"Well, what do you think might help you? What would you like to do about your situation?" I asked, hoping to direct her in a way that she could get through some of her huge anger.

"There's nothing I can do," she came back. "I got taken. He's gone and living in Mexico. He went down there with his new woman right after we split. I haven't seen him and I don't want to. So I'm stuck here. I just should have known better.

"People try to tell me I should forget about him and move on with my life. My friends say, 'Amy! He's gone! Okay, he was awful! But quit thinking about him. The only way the guy is still creating problems for you is in your own mind! You're choosing to keep your anger alive and well, and, are you ever doing a good job!'

"They just don't understand. He was *really* awful. He's the one that needs to change, not me." She sat quietly for another minute, and then, as if lifting a familiar load, she stood up with effort, thanked me for listening, and made her way out the door with all that heaviness on her shoulders.

Like her friends, I could listen and listen but until Amy decides to let go of the blaming and admit her own deep sorrow, she will be tied to her grief.

YOU CAN'T PREVENT BIRDS OF SORROW FLYING OVER YOUR HEAD—BUT YOU CAN PREVENT THEM FROM BUILDING NESTS IN YOUR HAIR.

Chinese proverb

A Daughter's Gift

"She was my treasure. She was the one good thing I've contributed to this world. Such a fine young woman! People would tell me all the time how wonderful she was. Whenever I doubted myself, whenever I felt down and depressed, the way I'd get out of it was to think of her. I'd think, 'I brought a wonderful person into this world. I can't be useless, or of no value. Something about me is good.'

"But when she died, it felt like I died, too. It felt like life died, like the whole world was different. Nothing made sense anymore and there was no reason for anything. It was by far the worst time of my life. Never had I gone through anything like it, and there was no way out. It was like I lost everything I had. I can't even remember a lot about that time except that I was more miserable than I dreamed anyone could ever be, and then I was just numb, in a daze.

"Some days I wouldn't get out of bed. At first friends would come over, or call me, and try to help me.

But after awhile they gave up. I don't blame them. All I did was moan and cry. It felt like everything had ended. There was no reason for me to get up or do anything. I didn't eat. I wasn't sleeping. I was a mess.

"I really don't know how I survived. I had absolutely no reason to go on that I could think of. No reason. Somehow now I know that my whole sense of being alive was tied to my daughter. When she died, nothing else was there."

It was hard to imagine the attractive, vibrant woman before me as the person she was describing. Well-dressed, obviously involved and busy with life, she had come up to me at a gathering when she heard of my interest in grief. She wanted to tell me her story, "in case it would help somebody else," she said.

"It was four years ago that the accident happened," she began, when I asked her about her daughter's death. "She was twenty-six and beautiful. She had finished school, had a degree in business and had been hired by a good company that really saw the potential in her. She had her own place and was in a serious relationship that was probably leading to marriage. But we were close as mother and daughter, too. We made a point of spending some time together every week. I was just so proud of her.

"She was going home late one evening from a girls' night out with some of her friends, and a car ran a stop sign and broadsided her. She died at the scene. The cops said she never knew what hit her. The guy had too much to drink and was driving too fast. She probably didn't even see him coming.

"When they finally called me it was early morning. I couldn't believe it. I kept screaming 'NO!' It was almost like somebody else was screaming. I was hearing my voice from a distance, like it wasn't mine. I kept asking where she was. I wanted to see her. They didn't want me to, but I had to. So somebody took me to her. But there was my beautiful daughter, my life, my hope for everything good. I can't describe what it was like seeing her there.

"It felt like the end for me. I don't know how I made it through the funeral and all. I just gave up. There was no point, no purpose in being alive. People tried to help me, they even took turns coming over to my place to see that I ate and that I was okay. I wasn't very nice to them. I wasn't okay, and nobody could make me okay.

"I got angry with all of them. They didn't know what it was like to lose a daughter, a precious daughter who meant the whole world, everything to me. Those weren't just words. I meant it. It was no use living without her. I thought about killing myself. I wanted to die and be with her. I even started thinking how I could do it. But I didn't even have enough energy for that. And then I worried that if I killed myself and went to hell for it, I'd never see her again. I was in a hole, and there was no way out.

"So I lived in an awful state for more than two years crying all the time. And the sad thing was, I didn't want it to change. It was like I had made a decision that nobody was going to make me be any different than I wanted to be. And I wanted the world to know that I had had a terrible blow. I knew things were never going to get any better, and I resented anyone who tried to make me think differently. When I think about it now, it's a miracle that I still have any friends left. My sister came really close to giving up on me, but somehow she's still around.

"You'll never guess who made me get myself out of that awful place I was wallowing in and move on with my life. Of all people, it was my daughter. Well, and my sister had something to do with it too. One day my sister was with me, and I was in my usual state of crying to her and telling her how much I missed Julie, and how I couldn't bear the thought of life being like this for the rest of my days, and on and on. And out of the blue, she said to me, 'Jan, if Julie could be here right now, listening to you and seeing what you're doing and how you're living, what do you think she'd say to you? You two were close; you know what she'd say. What would it be?'

"You could have blown me away. It was like Julie was right there for a minute. I could see her! And I knew exactly what she'd say. She would have said, 'Mom, what on earth are you doing? I'm really sorry that you had to experience me dying, but you're the one that always told me about making the best of things. How do you think I ever got to where I did in my life? You taught me a good lesson, but now you're not doing it yourself. What's with you, Mom? Get on with it.'"

Jan choked up then with the memory. As she dabbed at her eyes with a tissue, she said, "That did it. That was my turning point. It was awful to lose her, and I'd give anything to have her back. But I can't. I see now that it would be no gift to her or me or anyone else for me to live out my life like I'm already dead, or in the miserable way I was doing it. It was almost like I was trying to punish somebody.

"One other thing struck me about my experience. It hasn't been easy. I still miss her more than I can say. But what I try to do now is to share my life with her. I talk to her sometimes when something good happens and ask her to share it with me. And sometimes that makes me enjoy it all the more. And when something hard happens, I ask her advice. And it's amazing how many times some idea will come that helps me out. Who knows where it's coming from? Of course, I do know. It's from Julie."

WHOEVER IS STIFF AND INFLEXIBLE IS A DISCIPLE OF DEATH. WHOEVER IS SOFT AND YIELDING IS A DISCIPLE OF LIFE.

Tao Te Ching

1 0

Begin Building New Life on the Cornerstone of Loss

WITH THE BREAKDOWN OF WHAT
HAS GONE BEFORE THE POSSIBILITY
OF REBIRTH COMES.

Marion Woodman and Jill Mellick

In the pattern of this universe, loss and death are essential to the cycle of life. We've spent so much of our lives running from loss, working to avoid it, that we may miss this truth: new birth and new life is always preceded by loss and death.

Looking back on our lives we often find hidden in our painful losses the seeds that became new life, new growth for us. "I was furious," JoAnn remembered, "when after my husband died somebody said to me that I'd 'grow through this experience.' I could have strangled her. So that was supposed to console me? What an awful thing to say at a time like that! And yet, there was some truth in those words. I always used to be scared to do anything for myself. I didn't think I knew enough, or could do it well enough. But not having Tom here to do things for me showed me that I could. I had to. I still wish he was here, but I do see that in some ways I am stronger."

Opportunities to find new life are always present but, like JoAnn, when we're so caught up in our sadness and grief, it may take a while for us to see them. And early in our grief, understandably, the last thing we tend to look for is the possibility of new life.

Throughout our years of maturing, many steps in our development ask us to let go of where we've been and move on to the next stage. When we're little we don't feel the pain of these steps, of what we're leaving behind, because we're so eager to grow up. But as we age, we often experience how hard it can be. We may not think of these natural losses as needing to be grieved, and yet that's exactly what we should do. The bereavement enables us to move more easily on to the next place in our development.

Just as new growth in a plant requires pushing its way up through the dark and heavy soil to break through to light and new life, so the goal of our grieving is also a movement toward light and new life. We must look for the light though. Sometimes new life comes and hits us over the head, but many times the light shines through in unexpected ways. We may also miss opportunities for new life because we're not looking for them.

Barbara was telling us about her eight-year-old son who was inconsolable after his father died. Timmy closed up and refused to talk about his dad or his feelings. No matter what anyone tried—direct questioning, loving closeness, counseling help—Timmy remained withdrawn. The family worried. No one knew how to break through to this little boy whose world was destroyed when his daddy died.

Tim's dad, an avid outdoorsman, had been climbing high in the mountains when he slipped and fell off a steep slope. No one knew exactly where he landed, and he was missing for almost a week. Finally, a search and rescue team found his body and returned it to the family for burial. Weeks after the funeral, Timmy was closed up in his own world while his family, struggling with their own deep grief, worried about him.

Then one day, Tim came to his mom and said that he wanted to ask her a question. "Of course, honey," she said, hugging him close to her, hoping that somehow she could ease his great sorrow.

"Mom," Timmy began, his request marking the turning point in his grief, "I want to meet the dog that found my dad."

The life-death-life cycle had taken another small turn in the direction of life again. Sometimes the turn occurs through the companionship of animals, or other lessons from the natural world often offer opportunities for new life. Animals, for example, seem to have some understanding of a person's feelings. Carol told the following story: "I was so sad and not sleeping well that one afternoon I sat on the couch, crying my eyes out, and as I quieted down I fell asleep. I think I slept at least a half hour, and when I woke up Buffy had her head on my lap and was just standing there with me like she was taking care of me. She was a very sensitive dog and really close to me. I know she knew how I felt. It was so good to have her there."

A man whose wife was quite ill for a long time said, "My horses got me through it. I could just go and be with them, or ride without saying a word, and they kept me whole."

There are other seemingly random events that also speak directly to us and stimulate new thinking or new directions for us. Sharon was devastated by the shooting death of her husband in an attempted robbery while he was on a business trip in another state. She felt totally unable to go on and care for their two young children. She felt like she was just stumbling through life and couldn't handle it much longer. A few months later she was at church and, in her loneliness, just happened to strike up a conversation with an older woman.

Some months later when the older woman died, Sharon sent a note to the family telling how their mother had profoundly affected her life. "I was lost," she wrote. "I just thought I couldn't make it without my husband. And then I met your mother, who knew nothing about me. But in our conversation she told me how she was widowed in her thirties with five young children, and about some of the things that got her through. We talked and talked, and I told her about my husband, and I came away thinking that if she could do it, so could I. It was a turning point for me, and I want you to know how much she helped me."

Finding something that triggers new life may come from words in a book that seems to directly speak to you or from an old friend who passes through town and calls to see how you are. Opportunities that steer us toward new life come to us in all sizes and shapes and from all directions. It's up to us to notice them and choose to respond.

DEATH IS ALWAYS IN THE PROCESS OF INCUBATING NEW LIFE, EVEN WHEN ONE'S EXISTENCE HAS BEEN CUT DOWN TO THE BONES.

Clarissa Pinkola Estes

Begin Building New Life on the Cornerstone of Loss

- Call to mind some of the losses of your own life, and consider what growth may have come through them.
- Can you remember any situation when a random event or experience brought you blessing or growth? In what ways that you least expected did your experience offer you opportunities that pushed you toward new life?
- How have animals or nature played a significant role in your life? Do you find healing moments with them?

BIRTH IS NOT ONE ACT; IT IS A PROCESS. THE AIM OF LIFE IS TO BE FULLY BORN, THOUGH ITS TRAGEDY IS THAT MOST OF US DIE BEFORE WE ARE THUS BORN. TO LIVE IS TO BE BORN EVERY MINUTE. DEATH OCCURS WHEN BIRTH STOPS.

Erich Fromm

Grief Delayed

My mother died in 1995 when I was forty-three years old. I was unable to grieve for her, at least in the sense of experiencing pain and loss. Her final illness had been a dreadful struggle with chronic lung disease, and the only emotion I felt at the time of her death was relief. I shed no tears. The lack of pain astonished me. Although my relationship with her was difficult, I loved my mother and always assumed her death would be an overwhelming experience.

About a year after she died, I was cleaning a closet in her house and found four boxes of letters that had passed between my parents and me during my undergraduate years. I had filed them away long ago, one box for each year, and forgotten them. As soon as I recognized what they were, curiosity overcame me, and I stopped my work to sit down and read them.

My mother was an alcoholic. Her drinking began when I was a child and progressed over time, gradually at first, then becoming markedly worse after I entered graduate school. As a result, I often felt that she was a different person at different stages of my life: loving and gentle when I was a small child, distracted but kind during my adolescence and college years, and then increasingly angry, self-destructive, and abusive after I reached adulthood. Over time drinking destroyed my mother's character—a greater tragedy than physical extinction—and I had shed many tears over her in the course of that type of death within life. The last fifteen years had been so bad that I had nearly forgotten the person she had been when I was younger. In the end, I saw to it that she got the best medical care, but held her at an emotional distance. She had seemed almost a stranger. Indeed by the time of her death the mother I knew as a girl and young woman had long been gone.

In the letters, however, I encountered Mother again. The person who came through was warm, generous, full of sensible advice. She wanted to help me and had a much broader perspective than I did on whatever challenge I was dealing with at the time. Though she wanted me to do well in the sense of fulfilling my potential, she clearly cared about *me*, not about what I achieved in the way of grades, honors, or social success. In many ways then, she was an ideal mother.

Meeting her again on the page provoked a storm of emotion. I sat reading her letters and sobbing for several hours. I realized that I had indeed lost my mother, that she would never come back, and that she had been my best and truest friend. Thus I experienced a volcanic upheaval of pain that had been stored within, beneath scar tissue that sealed it off from consciousness. I felt as though I were being split open as it emerged. Suddenly I recognized that I was somehow in the throes of giving birth.

"What am I giving birth to?" I asked. "Myself," came the answer. As the pain rose out of the depths, I felt that I was being reborn. Parts of me that had been dead or dormant for years were being revived: the capacity for emotion, which had subsided as I numbed myself and tried to "deal objectively" with Mother; my relationship with her, which had also been sacrificed in the interest of emotional survival; and the sense of sharing any common life or purpose with her, even though I had modeled myself on her as a child.

Michie Hunt

WE JOURNEY THROUGH THE LABYRINTH OF OUR SOULS. THE MYSTERY LURES US INTO DEATH, WHICH LEADS US INTO LIFE.

Marion Woodman and Jill Mellick

Three Otters

*The same incident may speak differently to different people,
or there may be similarities. Rarely are our experiences or
perceptions exactly the same. The following two stories are
how the same incident after a family tragedy was experienced
individually by the husband and wife. They are each true
examples of life flowing from loss.*

On May 12, 2000, my husband Kevin received news
that our fifteen-year-old son, Ben, was missing
after having spent the night at a friend's house along
the Snake River. Later he learned that a person of Ben's
description had been seen and heard calling for help in
the turbulent spring runoff.

I had left town for the weekend and was called
Saturday night and told of the current situation. Under
the care of my good friend, Ann, we drove through the
night, returning to my anxious family. Kevin and I prepared ourselves to join the search and rescue efforts at
8:30 a.m. Sunday morning. We arrived at the designat-
ed meeting spot to join with thirty to forty members of
our local search and rescue team, some of whom had
been our friends and neighbors for many years.

From a high bank, fifty or sixty feet above the river,
we watched with J.C., our assigned trauma specialist,
an actively churning eddy. We watched anxiously as
rafts were shuttled to the eddy area where search dogs
had indicated the first scent. We stared at the water for
nearly two hours in hopes of somehow catching a
glimpse of Ben's body surfacing in the dirty spring
runoff. Later we heard the call come over J.C.'s radio
that Ben's body had been found about ten miles
downstream.

This wonderful river, in whose carved valley I had
grown up, took on a whole new meaning. Never again
would my primary associations with the river be a
place where so many wonderful friendships had

grown, where I had skinny-dipped as a teenager, and where we had built sandcastles and had picnics on hot summer days. The river was now frighteningly powerful, dark and angry, taking trees, rocks and an innocent young life that got in its way.

Each day coming and going to work, I'd cross the dark, powerful river's bridge, and each time I'd be haunted by the great power beneath me, which had pushed the air from breathing lungs and caused a body to become bruised, swollen, and lifeless.

Three days later we held a memorial and made plans to scatter Ben's ashes on his birthday some two months later when the snow would have melted at Grassy Lake. The week prior to the ash scattering, Kevin and I were anxious and uncertain how to go about the task. Neither of us had been back to the eddy, nor had our seven-year-old daughter Chantel been to the location where Ben was last seen.

Searching for some closure, we decided to return to the eddy. With Chantel in tow, we drove south after work one evening. We stood above the river speculating how Ben must have climbed down the steep embankment, how the water had changed as the spring became summer. We observed the peaceful surroundings for maybe fifteen minutes.

I had turned and begun to walk back to the car, when Kevin exclaimed,

"Jana, come here, look!"

In the calm above the eddy, along the far shore, were three of the largest river otters I'd ever seen. They rolled, played, swam, and entertained us in the graceful way that only an otter can. We watched through binoculars as they swam, rolling playfully from backs to stomachs, climbing out onto the smooth rock outcropping and slipping back into the water, all this time staying carefully above the eddy, as if they knew to be cautious. Then as the grand finale, one of them cautiously rode the current along the outer edge of the eddy, dove down, and sprang up right in the center, then quickly returned to the calmer waters above with the other two.

This dramatic act of nature consoled us. It restored in us the rhythms and the soothing power of the river. Once more, we had regained peace with the river.

Jana Roice

The week of the spreading of Ben's ashes—July 22, two days before his birthday—Jana decided we ought to re-visit the site of his drowning, as we'd been intending to do. We hadn't been there since his body was found on May 14. We went on Thursday, July 20, after Jana got home from work. We got a late start, and it was getting well on toward sunset when we arrived at the spot that is upstream from the Astoria Hotsprings Bridge.

We were across the river at approximately the same place we'd been watching on May 14 as Search and Rescue had used boats and search dogs to determine if Ben was still trapped in the whirlpool that perpetually circles there. The site of the whirlpool is on the downstream side of two large, flat rocks, like shelves, or steps fashioned for giants, that jut out into the river. Ben had last been seen by witnesses both on these rocks and then in the whirlpool on the downstream side.

The water was much lower now, of course, and the whirlpool seemed relaxed, gentle, non-threatening, from our vantage point high above and across the river. You could even see the bottom of the main part of the riverbed. It's a very beautiful spot, quiet and contemplative, which even the traffic of the highway cannot disturb.

We were standing there looking at that stretch of the river, just getting ready to leave. Suddenly we caught a flash of a dark shape climbing onto the lower of the two flat rock ledges that were the upstream wall of the whirlpool. We watched the shape, and two others appeared, all three coming out of the river onto the rocks. Through binoculars these creatures were clearly identifiable as otters.

There was a larger one and two smaller ones, rolling and playing, eating a fish, and generally having a great time. We watched them for probably a half-hour, goofing on the rocks, eating that fish, and even swimming in the whirlpool that had taken Ben's life.

It was an incredible sight, and strangely compelling, because there were exactly three otters. Not two, not four, three. Rare and wonderful.

Passing a message from Ben to us? It was easy to feel that way. Our thoughts have returned to that quiet celebration of life many times.

Kevin Roice

AND SO LONG AS YOU HAVEN'T EXPERIENCED THIS: TO DIE AND SO TO GROW, YOU ARE ONLY A TROUBLED GUEST ON THE DARK EARTH.

Goethe

1 1

Invite Compassion to Help You Heal

As you grow in light and clar-
ity, the pain of others becomes
transparent to you . . . and
your heart is always open in
love and grief for everyone.

Andrew Harvey
and Mark Matousek

When we open our eyes to the way things are in this world, we discover that no one is immune from loss and suffering. We come to see that, along with all its beauty and gifts, the world also contains sickness and old age, hunger and war, loss and death in count-less guises. Our own losses and distress may be instru-mental in waking us to the fact that we aren't alone in our suffering. We share the experiences of loss, pain, and death with all other beings in the world. This awareness itself can help us in our own grief.

When we are under assault from an important loss of our own, we tend to feel overwhelmed. Our first reaction is to pull into our center, gather our resources, and protect ourselves. In the early stages of grief, we tend to do something quite similar. Our world narrows down, we turn inward, and we are caught up in the intensity of our loss. We have little energy or interest in other concerns.

"Just after Jerry died I didn't even know what the weather was like," Cynthia confided. "The sky could have been falling in, and I wouldn't have known or cared. I was wrapped up in my own world. In fact, it took me quite a while to begin tuning into things again. It was like I was coming out of a fog."

Through the course of healthy grieving, this self-absorption gradually gives way to a keener awareness of being in the world without our loved one. We're torn between facing our loss head on and staying with the pain or withdrawing into our own dark places where we think we can avoid the pain. The choice we make here can be a step toward healing or refusing to heal.

We move toward healing when we choose to inch our foot out the door of our own grief and back into the day to day happenings of life. Then we can choose compassion for ourselves, but we can also begin to share in the suffering of others. As our own heart is opened and healed, it seeks the healing of what is around it. We may also grow in the awareness that we, through our own struggle with suffering and loss, can be the source of blessing for others. In the depths of ourselves we know their pain—not in its particulars, but in our common suffering.

Compassion is the ability to be moved in one's heart by the troubles of others. At its root, it means "to suffer with." To be compassionate means then to be conscious of the suffering of others, to be moved by their distress, and to desire to ease or alleviate their suffering. Grief over the death of a spouse or of a friend makes it difficult for us to see outside the darkness of our pain. If in our feelings of compassion we can extend a hand outside the pain to help someone, to be with them in their suffering, we may just be pulled into light again.

The famous psychiatrist, Dr. Karl Menninger, lectured a group of mental health professionals and then asked for questions. Someone in the audience asked what he would do if a client came to him and said that he felt a nervous breakdown coming on. Menninger's listeners expected him to advise immediate psychiatric help. Instead, he said he would tell the client, "Lock up your house, go across the railway tracks, find someone in need and do something to help that person."

Menninger understood that compassion is a two-way street. The giver receives and the recipient gives. As one person commented about hugs, "The wonderful thing about hugging somebody else is that you get one too!" So the grieving person who reaches out in compassion is often also consoled.

Suffering does not need to be sought out, however, so that we can become more compassionate. Enough suffering and grief happen to us in life's course of events to give us plenty of fuel for compassion. But the point is that the pain of our grief, unwelcome as it is, can have the effect of sensitizing us to the pain of others. Our grief offers an opportunity for insight, growth, and compassion. One of the fruits of compassion is the healing of our own grief.

Stories told by people who are suffering often speak of the simple presence of another, of the willingness to share their pain. One terminally ill patient said, "What helps me the most is when people try to understand what I'm feeling." Another said, "Just sit here with me and let me hold your hand. It helps when someone is close." Grief groups are often great sources of help as compassion for each other flows from one person to another.

These opportunities to reach out and share the pain of another are offered in losses other than death. A business executive who lost her job due to downsizing reached out in her own grief to the person who had given her the bad news, and said, "I'm so sorry you've had to do this. It must be terrible for you." She was amazed when her old boss broke down in tears and told her how much she hated being the one to bring such pain into other people's lives.

We humans seem to have been born with a natural gift that feels the suffering of others and wants to help alleviate it. Infants in nurseries tend to cry when other infants are crying. My neighbor, Janet, tells a story of her two sons, Leif and Eric, at ages two and three, who were told to sit in the corner after a bout of misbehavior. As they sat next to each other, Leif was most distressed, crying loudly, and begging for mercy. At the sound of his brother's great upset and apparent suffering, Eric, the younger of the two, took out of his own mouth the piece of candy he had managed to hold on to and put it into his older brother's mouth.

When we reach out of our own grief to bring comfort or help to others, we move toward assuaging the suffering of the world, and we become instruments of healing. Once we offer such loving compassion, we find that it flows in all directions, much of it returning to us in healing and wholeness.

WHAT A SPLENDID WAY TO MOVE
THROUGH THE WORLD, TO BRING
OUR BLESSINGS TO ALL THAT WE
TOUCH.

Jack Kornfield

Invite Compassion to Help You Heal

- Consider how compassionate you are with yourself. The assault of grief asks that we be gentle with ourselves, treat ourselves lovingly. Do your expectations of yourself allow that gentleness?

- Compassion for yourself asks that you set healthy limits on your own actions and that you nourish yourself well and open your heart to those who care for you. Think about how well you do these things.

- In what ways has your own grief acquainted you with the suffering and grief of others? Do you feel your kinship with others in our common struggles?

- How do you reach out in compassion to those in your own world who you know are suffering?

- What has your own suffering taught you about compassion? Have you been able to identify with others in the world you may not know: the hungry, the war-torn, the homeless, the grieving? How does that learning play out in your life? Does it invite any action on your part?

PARADISE IS HERE BUT IT CAN ONLY BE FELT WHEN ALL OF MORTALITY IS EMBRACED, WHEN ALL OF HUMANITY HAS BEEN GATHERED TO YOU AS BROTHERS AND SISTERS, WHEN YOU LIVE WITH THE PAIN OF TRUTH AND THE LOVE IT REQUIRES.

Andrew Harvey and Mark Matousek

A Mustard Seed

There is an old Chinese tale about the woman whose only son died.

In her grief, she went to the holy man and said, "What prayers, what magical incantations do you have to bring my son back to life?" Instead of sending her away or reasoning with her, he said to her, "Fetch me a mustard seed from a home that has never known sorrow. We will use it to drive the sorrow out of your life."

The woman set off at once in search of that magical mustard seed. She came first to a splendid mansion, knocked at the door, and said, "I am looking for a home that has never known sorrow. Is this such a place? It is very important to me." They told her, "You've certainly come to the wrong place," and began to describe all the tragic things that had recently befallen them. The woman said to herself, "Who is better able to help these poor unfortunate people than I, who have had misfortune of my own?"

She stayed to comfort them, then went on in her search for a home that had never known sorrow. But wherever she turned, in hovels and in palaces, she found one tale after another of sadness and misfortune. Ultimately, she became so involved in ministering to other people's grief that she forgot about her quest for the magical mustard seed, never realizing that the quest itself had in fact eased the sorrow in her own life.

YOU TAKE IT ALL IN. YOU LET THE

PAIN OF THE WORLD TOUCH YOUR

HEART AND YOU TURN IT INTO

COMPASSION.

Jack Kornfield

Carolyn's Rainbow

As Carolyn sat at Dave's bedside watching his labored breathing, she pondered, as she had many times before, the miracle that had brought Dave into her life. Still, at the same time, she wondered if she had not made a terrible mistake.

Two years before, because she was bored from the routine of retirement, Carolyn had gotten out of bed one Monday morning and called a phone number she had seen in the church bulletin the day before under the heading: "Needed: Mature People to Be AIDS Buddies." At the time, Carolyn thought it odd that this should be in the bulletin. But as she toasted her English muffin for breakfast, she decided to call the number just to find out what it was about. "Doggone it, I need something to get me going. There's life in this sixty-eight-year-old gal yet," she thought to herself.

Then an unspoken memory pierced her consciousness: the anguish of her friend Martha, whose son had died from AIDS, alone and uncared for. Martha would never forgive herself for having so alienated her son that they had severed all ties. Tears formed in Carolyn's eyes. "Too late, God, too late."

Carolyn signed on for the training. The training itself shocked some of her sensibilities. She had worked hard all her life and raised three kids, but she realized now that her world had been narrower than she imagined. She had never had to talk about her feelings about homosexuals, IV drug users, and hemophiliacs before. After the training she was assigned to be Dave's buddy.

The first meeting with Dave did not go well. From the outset Dave demanded more than what the simple assigned meeting called for. He was angry at Carolyn, Bill, the program coordinator, the clinic, the medical profession, gay people, straight people, the federal government—the world. Dave wanted someone to heap his anger on. Carolyn caught the brunt of his rage on the first visit. After absorbing an hour-long harangue, she left confused, mad, and hurt.

Even so, Carolyn gritted her teeth, determined to care for Dave. She thought about his gaunt looks, wasted body, shabby apartment, and loneliness. During his tirade Dave had complained about having to move back here from Chicago, about being deserted by his partner, and about his "useless, so-called friends."

Carolyn visited Dave about once a week during the first year. She cooked anything she could think of that Dave could keep down. Despite his persistent grumbling, Dave ate and even gained some color back in his cheeks. Gradually, Dave sprinkled stories about the pain of his parents' rejection, running away at age sixteen, drug addiction, recovery, and all the frustrated relationships he had been involved in. Carolyn began to see the warm, funny, clever sides of Dave.

Dave began having one infection after another. Even the new drugs had lost their effectiveness. Then he lost sight in one eye. Carolyn spent increasing hours with Dave. She often brought flowers to perk up the apartment. Once Carolyn had coaxed him into a support group, he began to have other visitors. She even managed to arrange a reconciliation between Dave and one of his sisters. And Dave and Carolyn talked.

Now he lay dying. Two months ago she had gathered his few belongings to bring to the nursing home. His sight had gone completely. He could no longer get out of bed and had extended lapses into semi-consciousness.

Most of the time Carolyn just came, plumped up Dave's pillows, and sat holding his hand. Her heart was breaking. She was losing someone who had grown to be a friend. One night, as Carolyn prepared to leave Dave, she leaned over and kissed his forehead. His hand tightened on hers.

"Thank you, Carolyn. You've given me more love than my mom ever did. I would've died long ago if it weren't for you. I love you so much. And, I had this dream," he stopped to breathe and swallow back tears. "When I'm in heaven, you'll see a rainbow and know I'm okay."

So now she waited. Grief would take its toll on her; she knew that. But she also knew that Dave had made the last two years of her life vivid, challenging, and alive.

A day later, Dave slipped away with a slight sigh. Carolyn helped Dave's sister arrange the funeral and the disposal of Dave's few possessions. A small group gathered at the graveside to mourn Dave's passing.

Sleep drew Carolyn into its silent embrace. She woke to the thunder and lightning of a fast-moving storm. When it passed, Carolyn crawled out of bed, dreading a day without Dave to care for. As she prepared coffee, she let her cat out the patio door. Turning to go back into the kitchen, off in the distance amidst the clouds, a rainbow arched across the bluing sky.

Carl Koch

GRIEF MELTS AWAY

LIKE SNOW IN MAY,

AS IF THERE WERE NO SUCH COLD

    THING.

WHO WOULD HAVE THOUGHT MY

    SHRIVELED HEART

COULD HAVE RECOVERED

    GREENNESS?

George Herbert

Ritualize Your Letting Go

AS HUMANS, WE FEEL A NEED TO PUNCTUATE OUR LIVES WITH CERE-MONIES TO MARK ENDINGS AND BEGINNINGS, UNIONS AND SEPARA-TIONS. A PERSONAL CEREMONY . . . SYMBOLIZES A PSYCHOLOGICAL, EMOTIONAL AND SPIRITUAL TRANS-FORMATION.

Lynda S. Paladin

Rituals and ceremonies have always played impor-tant roles in the lives of people from all cultures, historical periods, and upbringings. From the earliest times, people have always seemed to know that a ritu-al or ceremony helps us make our way through some noteworthy experiences, especially those marking changes in our lives.

We embrace formal rituals and ceremonies like grad-uations, weddings, christenings, bar mitzvahs, and funerals. We also celebrate ritually other experiences with baby showers, wedding showers, and birthday parties. Upon reflection, most of us could also discover some personal rituals of our own. One couple told me of a ritual they never miss: making their coffee and talking together each morning before they start the day.

Rituals allow us to act out our experience in some symbolic way and transition to another stage of life. As a bride and her father approach the groom, the ritual calls for the father to "hand over" his daughter to her future husband. The symbolism of this ritual gesture clearly marks a transition in the woman's life. She moves into a new family relationship. Indeed, most rituals and ceremonies combine symbolic actions with words, so that we fully engage ourselves in the experience.

Rituals can help us as we struggle with the loss of someone or something significant. Formal and informal ritualizing of our experience of loss can move us along in our healing. The wake and funeral after the death of someone dear are classic rituals that bring together all who are touched by the loss. The rituals encourage meaningful sharing and mutual support through a formalized structure.

People who have been divorced have often noted that one of the most difficult aspects of divorce is the lack of any formalized ritual to help them through their grief. Intense, painful emotions sometimes overwhelm the parties involved. Divorce is often as devastating as death. Because no formal ceremony marks the end of the marriage, people experiencing divorce often feel like they are existing in a state of limbo.

Rituals can be helpful in our healthy grieving because they allow us to express the loss that is so significant. Rituals help us to perform some action that gives form and movement to what we're feeling inside. They allow us to express the emotion that we often feel we must keep under wraps. The symbols we use are ways of focusing our feelings and thoughts. A ritual connects us with the person whom we've lost and helps us along with the change in our relationship.

Because of the uniqueness of each of us, of our relationships, and of our losses, we might find we can be quite creative in our grieving rituals. We can fashion a small ceremony—sometimes just for ourselves—that speaks to a particular aspect of our grief. And while formal ceremonies tend to happen early in our grief, we can create personal rituals that help us throughout the period of our grieving, each one addressing whatever we feel is prominent at that time.

In my own family, each year we all gathered at my mother's home for Christmas dinner. The year my mother died, Christmas came just five months after her death. So, we gathered at her home again, several of us preparing the meal. As we set the table, we placed two extra candles on it—one candle to represent our mother and one candle for our sister who had died several years earlier and whose children continued to celebrate with us. When we said our grace before the meal, we spoke of their presence and how we remembered them. Then we spoke of our gratitude to them for all they had brought to our family. It was a short ceremony, but one filled with love and remembrance.

Another family I know told me how sad they felt in the year after their father's death when his birthday rolled around. They were a family that celebrated birthdays with great fanfare. So, they decided to go ahead with a birthday party for their dad. They prepared all his favorite foods. As they shared the meal together, they also shared their memories of him.

In creating our own rituals for a deceased loved one, we can decide just how formal or informal we want to be. We might include singing, readings, or recordings of favorite music. We might compose the whole ritual ourselves, or simply gather with a purpose and create it as we go along. After the sudden and unexpected death of a young woman who was blessed with many friends and a big family, everyone gathered in her yard, a favorite place of hers. Each person held a candle and stood in a circle. When anyone wanted to contribute some memory or reading or comment, that person walked to the center of the group and spoke.

We can create quite unique family rituals that can become traditions we repeat over time. Throughout the time of our grieving, as we encounter and experience anniversaries, holidays, and other special times, our own rituals may be a great source of comfort and help in our sorrow.

EVEN THE SADDEST THINGS CAN BECOME, ONCE WE HAVE MADE PEACE WITH THEM, A SOURCE OF WISDOM AND STRENGTH FOR THE JOURNEY THAT STILL LIES AHEAD.

Frederick Buechner

Ritualize Your Letting Go

- Take some quiet time to sit and consider the rituals or ceremonies you already experience in your life, even those not connected with loss. Which are those that are quite significant to you?

- Think about the ways you feel "stuck" in your grieving. What ritual could you design, just for yourself, that could help you move along and smooth the progress of your grieving?

- Can you think of some symbols in your everyday life that represent your connection to whom or what you've lost? How do these symbols speak to you? What ritual could you build around one or more of these symbols?

- Create a ritual around giving away the belongings of someone who has died. For example, one widow put together some words of prayer and a statement to her husband who had died. As she gathered his favorite belongings to give away, she offered the prayer, then spoke to each item, saying something like, "Golf clubs, I give you, in Joe's name, to Tim. May you bring joy and pleasure to him, and be a source of good exercise and health."

- When you anticipate anniversary dates with some anxiety, create a celebration of that date, making it a significant and personalized experience.

- Conduct a candlelight ceremony to acknowledge your progress through your loss and grief. Note what is helping you survive and what is helping you thrive. Affirm the positive in yourself. Look for growth.

AS AN OUTWARD AND VISIBLE SIGN OF A CHANGE IN LIFE OR AN AFFIR-MATION OF BELIEF, CEREMONIES SYMBOLICALLY CONNECT US TO OUR BELIEFS AND OUR COMMUNITY.

Lynda S. Paladin

El Dia de Los Muertos

Maria and her brothers and sisters were devastated when their mother died. She had been the powerful force of the family for years. Abandoned by her husband with six small children, their mom knew there was only one thing to do—care for her family. So with little money and few resources, she always did what she could.

Through the course of their struggles together, the family grew extraordinarily close. What they had was each other, and they learned to rely on each other for everything. And their mother was at the center, always working hard, taking in laundry, cleaning houses, doing whatever she could to bring in a little money for her family.

As each child grew up and moved into adulthood, "Mama" remained important and close to each child. Now it was their turn to look out for her, especially as she got older and a bit unsteady. When Mama developed cancer, the whole family was devastated. They couldn't believe it and tried everything to make it not so. Surgery, chemotherapy, and radiation only brought short-term relief. Mama was the center of attention from all of her children who hovered and cared for her and attended to her many needs.

When Mama died, the family lost its anchor. They were like rudderless ships trying to make their way in a storm of grief. Connection to Mama and dependence on her still had enormous power over them, so they struggled with their grief. They had mixed feelings: some relief after the long cancer struggle, some guilt over the sense of relief, some feelings of inadequacy about getting along in the world without Mama, and some great sorrow to be left without their mother.

Feelings were so mixed, so ambivalent, that it was hard to make any progress with grief. And so the grieving went on for several years, fairly unchanged. For Maria, hard as it was to be in the world without Mama, she was ready to move on with her life. She knew she had to figuratively lay her mother to rest again.

One fall, when the cottonwood leaves were brilliant like the sun and the nip of coolness touched the nights, a possible answer came to Maria. The third anniversary of her mother's death had passed and Maria was musing about what made her mother happy in life. She was surprised when a picture of old Halloween nights came to her mind. Mama would build a big bonfire in the front yard, bring out candy and cookies, and enjoy the little ghosts, witches, and cowboys as they came trick or treating. It was a warm, happy memory. Now, Halloween wasn't far off.

Though their family had never celebrated *El Dia de Los Muertos*, the Day of the Dead, as they did in Mexico, Maria knew that this feast on November 2 was important to many of her relatives. It was a time to remember and reconnect with those who had died. So she set out to learn all she could and found books and stories about *El Dia de Los Muertos*.

In Mexican tradition, she learned, those who have died are given heavenly permission to visit with friends and relatives on earth. On the second of November, the whole country celebrates with fiesta, decorating graves with flowers and candles, bringing toys and food. The whole idea of the ritual is to remind each other that death is part of life.

Her ideas came together quickly as she read. She picked up the phone and called her brothers and sisters, nieces and nephews, and invited them to meet at the cemetery on Halloween. Each one was to bring some of what they knew was Mama's favorite food.

When the day arrived, Maria was prepared and went early to the cemetery. She had a wonderful time bringing flowers, candles, and food to the grave. A big, carved jack-o-lantern had a place of importance. She set a tablecloth just near her mother's headstone and placed candles around it. In the center she placed a skeleton mask she had bought, a reminder of those who had died, especially her mother. This was to be a celebration of her mother's journey that had taken her to its next stage and a time for the family to enjoy her and release her.

Family members began to arrive and couldn't believe the festive air. Each one came with "Mama's favorite food," but they were all different! Watermelon and cantaloupes, tortillas, beans and chili, big chocolate bars, a can of soda, and even a banana split appeared on the tablecloth near the headstone.

"We all sat on the ground around Mama's grave, and I read some of the things I'd picked up about this celebration," Maria recalled. "I reminded everybody that Halloween had always been one of Mama's favorite holidays, and that we were celebrating it with her. Even though she had died, she was still part of us, and her presence was still with us, even though she was now in a different form, on a different part of her journey.

"We each told why we brought the food we'd brought. We talked for a long time, telling all kinds of stories about Mama. Then my sister Rita put the skeleton mask on, wrapped herself in John's long overcoat, and started dancing around. It became a friendly mask, and pretty soon we had all taken turns putting it on, moving around the grave and in and out of everybody. Even the little ones did it.

"It was such a good time that nobody seemed to want to leave. It felt like we had sort of made peace with death. Everybody seemed closer together, and it felt like maybe Mama really did come back in her spirit that night, and spend time with us. We know that once you die your spirit still lives. And I think that Mama really enjoyed that time with all of us. It turned out that everybody decided we should do it every year, and so we do. It's our special celebration of Mama and her life with us."

RITUALS INVOLVE A NUMBER OF SPECIFIC HEALING PROPERTIES THAT CAN BE BENEFICIAL IN PROMOTING HEALTHY MOURNING.

Therese A. Rando

Memorial

The divorce had been angry and bitter, he had said, and the big man in uniform couldn't stop sobbing. The chaplain at the base in Germany happened upon him in the chapel one day and saw the shaking shoulders and bowed head. Touched by such apparent suffering, the chaplain had gone to him and asked if he could help. The gentle and genuine caring triggered the big man's flood of words and tears.

As they sat in the privacy of the chaplain's office, the anguish of the past months came out in a mixture of sadness, anger, and frustration and a sense of failure. Tom had entered the marriage with lots of love and expectations that he and Beth would have a solid future together. They talked of a family and settling down when his stint in the Army was over.

"I met Beth when I was in basic training, and she was working in the office on the base. She was a couple years younger than I was, really beautiful, and so much fun to be with. We just knew we had to be together and moved fast to get married. We had a great time for about a year. When I was being shipped out to Germany, she wasn't too happy about it, and we started fighting some. When I look back at it now, I see that I wasn't really aware of what she wanted. Actually, we didn't really know much about each other at all." Tom stopped for breath and shifted around in his chair.

"Well, to make a long story short, things got worse and worse. She did come with me here, and I thought maybe being in a foreign country would bring us closer together. But it had just the opposite effect. She didn't want to go to work or anything and spent a lot of time alone during the day. It was like she was just waiting to pounce when I came home. We fought and fought with only a few good times in between. It got uglier all the time, and we said awful things trying to hurt each other. I knew it was over, but I kept trying to hold onto what was just a dream."

Tom stopped talking for a minute or two, took a deep breath and looked like he was trying to decide whether to go on. The chaplain said, "It sounds like things were really tough for both of you. I presume that's when you went for the divorce? I know divorce can really be painful."

A new flood of tears erupted with a huge sob. "That wasn't the worst part of it. The divorce is not what's keeping me this way. Maybe something's wrong with me, but I just can't get over this." Tom had to wait a few minutes till his tears abated.

"Just before we finally called it quits, we were fighting and Beth screamed at me something I hadn't known. I know she wanted to hurt me, but I didn't know how much it would keep me like this." He stopped for a minute and looked at the chaplain, as if seeking something that would take the pain away. "She told me she had been pregnant and didn't want my baby, so she had an abortion." The words came out in a rush and were followed by deep, racking sobs.

They sat in a surprised and aching silence as the words hung in the air. Nothing had indicated this twist of events and the chaplain was taken aback at the pain humans inflict on each other. He felt helpless.

As Tom's sobbing slowed, he continued his story in short bursts. "Now I don't know what to do. That was my baby. That may have been the only baby I'll ever have in this world, and it didn't even have a chance at life. She didn't even tell me she was pregnant. The baby is the worst part of this whole thing, and I can't get over it. It's been a couple months now that I've known, and I can't shake it.

"Well, this may sound silly or stupid to you, Padre, but I got to the point where I had to do something, so I went out to the cemetery and walked and walked around, and cried a lot. And then, I came on a baby's grave. I have no idea who the baby was, or anything about it, but I started treating it like it was where my baby was buried. I go there a couple times a week, whenever I can, and I talk to my baby. I don't even know if my baby was a boy or girl, but I just tell the baby of my love. Sometimes I stay there a long time just talking. That helps some, but I've heard that I'm gonna be shipped out in a few weeks and it feels terrible to leave the baby there. I don't know how I can do that."

Tom was quiet now, his emotion having poured out with his story. He and the chaplain sat in that warm feeling that often marks the sharing of such an intimate and personal experience. The chaplain felt at a loss, as he so often did when human suffering came to him in the guise of a vulnerable person. And he prayed quietly for help.

Finally, he asked, "Tom, what would you think if you and I put together a memorial service for your baby? We can create it ourselves. You have a very unique situation, and we can create a very unique ceremony to lay your baby to rest and to bring you some peace."

And so they did. Together Tom and the chaplain, using a few parts of a child's funeral service, along with some personal and unique ideas from both of them, created a memorial service for Tom's baby. When they got the program, the candles, the readings, and the prayers together, they went out the next weekend to the gravesite that Tom had been visiting and had a beautiful and touching ceremony of love and surrender.

Two years later this chaplain shared his story with me, telling me how touched he was by Tom's plight and how helpless he felt in the face of his pain. Then he asked if I thought he had "handled it right." Before I told him how loving, empathic, beautiful, and creative I thought he and Tom both were, and how lucky I thought Tom was that he had found this chaplain, I asked if he'd ever seen or heard from Tom again.

A huge smile crossed his face. "A month ago, after having been away for the past two years, Tom came back to Germany and stopped to see me. He looked good to me. His face wasn't as lined with pain as I had remembered him. I asked him how he was doing.

"He paused a minute, and I could see a flash of the pain I remembered, and then his voice came with some resignation, 'Padre,' Tom said, 'We did good. It's still a very painful memory for me, and I get sad when I think about the whole experience, mostly so sad about the little one I never had a chance to know. But I think we laid him to rest in peace, and I think he knows of his dad's love for him. And that brings me some peace. And because of all that we did, I know my baby's little spirit is with me, wherever I go.'"

HE WHOM WE LOVE

AND LOSE

IS NO LONGER

WHERE HE WAS BEFORE.

HE IS NOW WHEREVER WE ARE.

John Chrysostom

JOAN GUNTZELMAN holds a Ph.D. in counseling psychology from the University of New Mexico and a master's degree in clinical psychology from Xavier University in Cincinnati. She has written numerous articles and several books on dealing with loss, including *124 Prayers for Caregivers*.

As a clinical assistant professor in the department of psychiatry at the University of New Mexico School of Medicine, and a general counselor with a private practice, Guntzelman often presents lectures and workshops to professionals in the medical field and other caregivers on how to deal with loss and adjust to the stresses of their jobs. She also directs Ring Lake Ranch, a not-for-profit, non-denominational retreat center in the Wind River Mountains of Wyoming that provides seminars and discussions for spiritual renewal. Guntzelman lives in Albuquerque, New Mexico.